Dr. DEATH
DR. JACK KEVORKIAN'S
Rx : DEATH

(Top) During one of many news conferences orchestrated by his chief counsel, Geoffrey N. Fieger (right), Dr. Jack Kevorkian watches his attorney toss barbs at prosecutors.

(Bottom) Dr. Kevorkian is escorted into court wearing jail garb by a deputy sheriff while Fieger's partner, Michael Alan Schwartz, prepares to defend the doctor on another charge of assisted suicide.
Photos by RICHARD HUNT

DR. DEATH

DR. JACK KEVORKIAN'S
RX: DEATH

JOAN BROVINS & THOMAS OEHMKE

LIFETIME BOOKS

Library of Congress Cataloging-in-Publication Data

Manufactured in the United States of America
1 2 3 4 5 6 7 8 9 0

Brovins, Joan M.
    Dr. Death: Dr. Jack Kevorkian's RX death / by Joan Brovins &
Thomas Oehmke.
        p. cm.
    Includes bibliographical references and index.
    ISBN 0-8119-0782-1
    1. Terminally ill—Case studies. 2. Pathologists—United States-
-Biography. 3. Right to die—Case studies. 4. Assisted suicide-
-Case studies. 5. Kevorkian, Jack. I. Oehmke, Thomas H.
II. Title. III. Title: Doctor Death.
R726.B765 1993
364.1'523—dc20
[B]
                                                        93-30345
                                                        CIP

PLEASE NOTE

This book contains what are thought to be real life and death events. The facts are gathered from interviews with the survivors and their friends, court documents, evidence admitted at judicial hearings, videotapes, news articles, stories and television newscasts.

The ideas presented are substantially and materially the same as those which have appeared in these referenced materials. Some quotations have been edited to facilitate clarity, brevity and story flow; nevertheless, all quotations are substantially and materially the same as spoken or reported to have been spoken.

Though interviewed twice briefly, due to competing demands on his time and a personal desire to remain apart from any commercial ventures associated with his efforts, Dr. Jack Kevorkian elected not to make himself available, instead, instructing that all contact be through his attorneys; Dr. Kevorkian's attorneys similarly declined to be involved.

Dedication

To those who have struggled with assisted suicide

like Prometheus, stealing fire from the gods

and willing to pay the price.

Table of Contents

ix

Table of Contents

Table of Contents

xi

Table of Contents

Prelude

In the United States, more than 4,000 end-of-life decisions are made each and every day. Doctors have been very quietly assisting patients in death for as long as there have been doctors. Every day, doctors write the prescription and whisper the recipe for deadly overdoses. They call it *mercy killing*. One of five doctors surveyed admitted to helping cause the death of a patient.

Thousands of people hope that Jack Kevorkian, M.D. will offer them the prescription to relieve their misery - - *medicide*. Kevorkian is the proponent of euthanasia which means "good" or "happy" death. But Kevorkian offers more than passive euthanasia, such as the voluntary withdrawal of artificial life-support for terminal patients.

Kevorkian practices *obitiatry*. Obitiatry is the practice of planned death and Jack Kevorkian, M.D., *obitiatrist*, is its practitioner. What had been a matter of whispered conversation for years was to become his distinctive style of "practicing medicine."

GALILEO AND ST. THOMAS MORE

Kevorkian has touted that ". . .reason and common sense were at last able to break the strangle hold of philosophical tyranny which branded suicide an unforgivable sin. . . ."

Prelude

Kevorkian notes that "the first blow was struck over 400 years ago by Thomas More, who in his classic, *Utopia*, proclaimed the right of suffering humanity to benefit from both active and assisted suicide. . . . Official opposition to active euthanasia from the Roman Catholic church displays egregious inconsistency. Thomas More himself was Catholic . . . raised to sainthood in 1935."[1]

It was this same church, at an Inquisition Court in 1663, which had condemned Galileo. The astronomer -- contrary to then-church teaching -- preached that the Earth revolved around the Sun. Incorrectly, the church had indoctrinated the faithful that the Earth, not the Sun, was the center of the Universe.

Though Galileo was right all along, the inquisitors had condemned him as a heretic. Found guilty of violating then-erroneous church doctrine, the Inquisition Court sentenced Galileo to life imprisonment, later reducing his sentence to house arrest.

Four centuries later, in 1992 and after Vatican experts had studied the question for 13 years, Pope John Paul II finally got around to reversing Galileo's condemnation.

MODERN DAY PROMETHEUS

Kevorkian may fashion himself to be a modern-day Prometheus, the Greek mythological titan god whose name means forethinker. Prometheus wanted to promote civilization. Though fire was a means of survival, Zeus did not wish that mere mortals should benefit from fire. Heroically, Prometheus stole onto Mt. Olympus and filched Fire itself from Zeus.

Prometheus was not to escape undiscovered. Zeus was shocked to learn that the power of fire was no longer the exclusive domain of the gods, but had been taken away by Prometheus.

Prelude

To punish Prometheus for this theft, Zeus angrily chained him to a tremendous rock. Though a lesser god, Prometheus had an immortal liver. While mighty bonds restrained Prometheus, Zeus commanded an eagle to steadfastly persecute the bound Prometheus by pecking out his liver.

In excruciating pain, he would approach death. Then, his liver miraculously would replenish and grow again, allowing the relentless attack of the eagle to begin anew. Thus, Prometheus was punished for stealing fire from gods and bringing it to mortals, giving them means of survival, thus, fostering and preserving civilization.

So, too, Dr. Jack Kevorkian has stolen Death from the gods. As Prometheus was persecuted, so too Kevorkian may see himself as a martyr, prosecuted by the criminal justice system for practicing what he terms *medicide*.

Is Dr. Death a serial mercy killer? A mercenary profiting on the pain of others? A ringmaster for euthanasia, dancing with death? Or is Jack Kevorkian the Angel of Mercy, alleviating irreversible misery?

This is the modern allegory of Prometheus.

chapter one

Taboos and Rules

In the hot summer months of 1989, out-of-work pathologist Jack Kevorkian, M.D. could be seen scouring the aisles of lumber and hardware outlets, rummaging garage sales and perusing the local flea market. His profile was bony, his body lanky and lean. The almost-retired medical doctor was on the scavenger hunt of his life, doggedly pursuing small clock motors, parts from toys, tiny pulleys and chains, electrical magnets and switches. He was building the science experiment to end all science experiments.

Had you troubled Kevorkian for his business card it would have read:

JACK KEVORKIAN, M.D.

Bioethics and Obitiatry

SPECIAL DEATH COUNSELING

This was a man with a mission. He lacked sophisticated and expensive machine tools. In fact, he had little more than an ordinary household toolbox at his disposal: a small electric drill and a soldering iron.

At first, his revolutionary invention was little more than a contraption. But one prototype after another was constructed. A better switch here, a stronger clock motor there, a more powerful solenoid elsewhere. At last, the gizmo's internal mechanism was completed. Using scrap aluminum sheeting and bars, Kevorkian fashioned a shiny cover with an extended handle. Finally, a stand was built for bottles of intervenous solutions. For $30 or less, he had constructed a machine that could snuff life quickly, quietly and painlessly. The inventor christened his suicide machine the "Mercitron". In the end, Kevorkian has resolved, "I tried to change things with words. Finally I decided I had to do it with actions."

The catalyst for Kevorkian came in a 1989 battle undertaken by David Rivlin, a Farmington, Michigan quadriplegic who fought to have his respirator removed. When Rivlin's doctor refused to disconnect the breathing device, Kevorkian offered to assist, but Kevorkian's self-help invention was then too complicated for the paralyzed Rivlin.

"That's when I realized a machine was needed that would be simple enough for patients to operate themselves," Kevorkian concluded.

Kevorkian had always shunned overly complex approaches to otherwise simple problems. As a physician, Kevorkian urged his colleagues, where possible, to avoid a "'high-tech' approach [which] would seem to be ostentatious and wasteful frippery. . . ."[2]

Applying that same principle to the Mercitron, Kevorkian said, "There's nothing tricky about the Mercitron. Just a couple of solenoids, a couple of

2

switches and electromagnets. . . . I did it all with flea market parts," Kevorkian proudly proclaims.

On a cold spring day in 1990, Kevorkian walked with his Mercitron -- with its three dangling bottles and lethal trigger -- to the offices of Royal Oak, Michigan's *The Daily Tribune* petitioning for some publicity. Kevorkian greeted the reporter with his chilly, ungloved hand remarking, "Cold as a cadaver, eh?"

"My humor offends people, sometimes," Kevorkian admits, "because I use them as foils to amuse myself."

THE CHILD INSIDE

"What do you want to be when you grow up?" people would ask. Before attending The University of Michigan School of Medicine, Kevorkian always wanted to be a sports announcer. Baseball, in particular. "I really wanted to be a baseball announcer. I'd have been a great one -- better than [perennial Detroit Tiger's announcer Ernie] Harwell," Kevorkian reflected.

Often bored in elementary school in Pontiac, Michigan, Kevorkian boasts, "You know, they skipped me up a grade in 6th because I caused a teacher to cry. I was throwing paper wads and shooting at the clock. I was bothering others, see, and she couldn't control me." At wits end, Kevorkian's young teacher lowered her head to the desk and wept in frustration. The school principal remedied Kevorkian's boredom by booting him up to junior high where he was more challenged.

While young Kevorkian may have been fascinated by baseball, his friends saw him heading in another direction. "I first met Jack when we were just teenagers. We both belonged to a national Armenian youth organization. My club served kids living in the southwest Detroit area. Jack and his pals belonged to the club in Pontiac," recounted Mitch Kehetian, now editor-in-chief of *The Macomb Daily* of Mount Clemens, Michigan.

3

Kehetian remembers Kevorkian as a maverick from way back. "Even then, we knew Jack was headed for the field of medicine. Although [Jack] was the studious bookworm type, he also had a knack for story-telling," Kehetian remembers. "Unlike his legal counsel today, Jack was no loudmouth. But when he spoke, we listened."

By the early fifties, Kevorkian was a top medical student at The University of Michigan. The youthful, impractical and idealistic, 31 year old resident possessed a self-described ". . .zeal of commitment to . . . a righteous crusade -- a self-imposed mission involving diverse academic disciplines, directly or indirectly relevant to all strata of society." Kevorkian then promised himself to "challenge profound philosophical viewpoints and clash head on with enduring and powerful taboos."

". . .There was nothing to lose by aiming for the highest theoretical standard of which [one] is worthy, toward the pure idealism of naivete, *shooting for the moon*, so to speak. I decided not to compromise. . .," Kevorkian resolved.

As a young physician, Kevorkian might have characterized his ideal medical hero as "A medical doctor of proven competence in research, of undeniable compassion and dedication and of impeccable character. They are rare," Kevorkian wrote. To Kevorkian, only Dr. Albert Schweitzer comes to mind.

In contrast, Kevorkian believes that "In today's world, altruism in the dispensation of health care is close to mythical. (The strictly commercial profit motive is becoming increasingly dominant in routine medically practice, in surgery, in hospitals and in research; and money is beginning to dictate priorities.). . ."3

Reflecting back 40 years to his days as a student, Kevorkian claims, "I've always felt that people had this right to die since I was in medical school seeing suffer-

4

ing patients. I would shake my head and say, "Wow, why do we keep such people living?"

Kevorkian's mother was a homemaker, his father a self-employed excavating contractor. Both were conventional thinkers, supportive of their son, but often puzzled by his strange crusades.

As to the *Hippocratic Oath*,* Kevorkian says that "Hippocratic tradition represents a rational and compassionate resolution of the conflicting duties to alleviate pain and suffering on one hand and to prolong life on the other."[4]

"I never took the oath," Kevorkian swears, "and as far as I know it was never officially administered to my graduating class in 1952 at The University of Michigan. Indeed, it is now uncommon for any American medical faculty to insist that the oath be taken by graduating doctors. That alone renders suspect the hallowed oath's importance or relevance to modern medical practice."[5]

"Just as that [Hippocratic] oath never had any real meaning with regard to abortion," Kevorkian notices, "so too it's now irrelevant in the right-to-die debate."[6] "It's time for a society obsessed with *planned birth* to consider diverting some of its attention and energy from an overriding concern with longevity of life at all costs to the snowballing need for a rational stance on *planned death*," that is, the "purposeful ending of human life by direct human action."

The young Kevorkian undertook his planned crusade by penning an essay, proposing "a neat and very simple concept" involving death row inmates who would voluntarily undergo strictly-controlled, surgical depth, irreversible, general anesthesia, safe for the commercial harvesting of all usable body parts. Kevorkian argued ". . .in

---

* The Hippocratic Oath says, "I will give no deadly medicine to anyone ii asked, nor suggest any such counsel."

favor of a well-organized, open and legally regulated commercial market for human organs and tissues." Kevorkian viewed other doctors as "blasé and, on this issue at least, a socially criminal profession."[7]

The purpose of anesthesia was to allow medical experimentation, otherwise impossible to do on living humans. If the condemned's live body survived the experiment, then an executioner would cause ultimate death with an overdose of an anesthetic agent. Kevorkian wrote:

> *Here at last was an invincible argument for . . . procurement of precious vital organs in the best possible condition in order to save lives of several dying patients. . . . A single healthy condemned inmate could be the salvation of at least six doomed adults by offering two biologically robust kidneys, two "clean" lungs, a heart and a liver; and, in addition, save two more by donating a fresh pancreas and small intestines. That adds up to a total of eight lives, but the precious transfer of life and death need not end there. If the condemned's liver were surgically divided, then two dying infants could also be saved, raising to nine the number of lives salvaged by one inmate. And a bone marrow transplant could save a tenth patient.*[8]

In 1959, Kevorkian published some of these thoughts in the first of many articles in legitimate journals.[9] Kevorkian later reflected, "Oh, brother, I was naive." His brief essay proved to have grave consequences and would cost him his university residency. Kevorkian wrote:

Taboos and Rules

I was soon to experience for the first time in my life the enormous force of social, political and historical inertia which makes it almost impossible to implement seemingly radical change, to bridge the wide gap between rational theory and actual practice.

So, I was not caught by surprise when a staff professor and friend [Dr. Adam French, chairman of the Pathology Department] approached me, evidently charged with the odious task of giving me a rare ultimatum: either I drop the controversial death penalty campaign or leave the residency program at the university. The decision was not easy . . . I resigned . . . and became a third-year resident in pathology at Pontiac [Michigan] General Hospital.

Kevorkian later said that ". . .everything humans think or do is based on *relative ignorance*, not on relative knowledge."[10]

Exiled from the academic nirvana of Ann Arbor back to his hometown, at Pontiac General Hospital Kevorkian undertook new research: transfusion of postmortem human blood. That is, transfusions from dead donors to live volunteers. Kevorkian recalls his first transfusion:

We transferred more than half a pint into the volunteer and I said, "How do you feel?" When she told me she had a strange taste in her mouth, that she felt quite dizzy, I almost fainted myself, I was so scared. . . .As it turned out, the deceased had a fairly high alcohol level in her blood and the volunteer

7

who got the blood was feeling the effects of the alcohol.

Dr. Kevorkian's early days at Pontiac General Hospital were vividly recalled by Floyd P. Miles, Jr. While physicians at the Hospital typically were aloof to a lowly ambulance attendant like Miles (who now is an owner of Fleet Ambulance Company), "Not so with Dr. Jack. He would join us in the cafeteria," Skip Miles recollected, "eager to discuss inventions; Dr. Jack really wanted to invent something that no one else had thought of before.

"So along with my partner, Dick Rudlaff, we three brainstormed the idea of tear-string to open an envelope — like the old bandaids — so you wouldn't get a papercut on your finger getting the letter out. We were excited as we experimented for days with suture, glue and envelopes until our invention worked perfectly.

"Though he could have exploited our invention all on his own without us ever knowing, instead, Dr. Jack scrawled out a contract on a napkin, a sort of temporary agreement, to equally share any profits until he could get a more formal contract written up by a patent lawyer," Miles remembered. "Dr. Jack was as disappointed as anybody when the lawyer said the idea was not patentable."

In a different vein, Kevorkian later continued his crusade for organ retrieval where capital punishment is involved. Although neutral on the issue of capital punishment, Kevorkian believed that if humans are to be executed, they should be permitted to partake of real retribution through a transfer of undeniable value: organs for transplantation. Individual autonomy or self-determination should be the driving force behind the justified and necessary use of human organs:

Taboos and Rules

According to perhaps the most basic secular moral principle (i.e., autonomy or self-determination), an individual has absolute dominion over his or her body -- the right of decision about what will or will not be done with or to its parts. . . .

Extending that principle of autonomy further to his fellow physicians, Kevorkian wrote:

Personal autonomy, which is highly touted, should apply to physicians too. Each should be free to refuse to perform lethal injections; that is moral.

However, it is immoral for a physician to impede the will or action of colleagues who consider it their moral and professional duty to perform such injections. The later, like abortionists, are killers, but neither group are murderers, which make all the difference objectively.

The ancient tug and pull between religion and law presented a profound problem that intrigued Kevorkian who has argued:

Any religion ought to be irrelevant to the strictly secular doctor-patient relationship. After all, it is a medical problem that brings the patient to a doctor. If the patient has any religious qualms or constraints, he has consulted the wrong professional.

Kevorkian has further observed that, criss-crossing through this problem of assisted suicide. . .

. . .are divergent concepts of the importance and meaning of religion and law, of disease and health and of life and death. Such concepts are grounded firmly in a wide spectrum of subjectivity, scrutiny of which has taxed the greatest philosophical minds. . . .

The first obvious question is crucial: Which is the highest ideal and the greatest Good, religion or secular law?

MANY JOBS, MANY PLACES

After completing his residency at Pontiac General Hospital, Kevorkian took a year off to do research in Europe. He returned to work at Detroit's old Receiving Hospital.

"I asked them to let me work at night," Kevorkian recalled. "I made what I called Death Rounds. I used to joke about it. Once I made a black arm band and started walking around looking for anybody dying in the hospital." The young resident carried around an ophthalmoscope, peering into the eyes of the dying to determine the onset of death; once dead, of course, a patient can no longer be revived. Kevorkian found his death rounds both interesting and taboo. That's when he earned his nick-name: *Dr. Death.*

A MONASTIC LIFE

The sinewy, silver-haired Kevorkian lives in a no-frills, walk-up apartment with a view of Main Street in downtown Royal Oak, Michigan. His single bed mattress lies on the floor. He's remarkably fit, climbing trees and walking fences for fun. Kevorkian has been seen tooling around the front lawn of his attorney's vacation home on Oxbow Lake — practicing his golf swing.

Taboos and Rules

A lifelong bachelor, some 24 years ago Jack Kevorkian spurned the idea of marrying a young store clerk. She could not measure up to Kevorkian's requisite for self-discipline. More than that, her sister was considered to be promiscuous, something Kevorkian would not tolerate. She wasn't a perfect mate. Her goals, skills, station in life did not compliment his own. It wasn't worth trying.

With other women, Kevorkian couldn't tolerate the idea of their relationship someday ending. Regretting that he never married, Kevorkian laments, "That's shirking responsibility as a human being. From nature's standpoint, I'm immoral. So now, there's no one alive with my name. My male relatives were killed in Armenia and I never built a family." In the end, its Kevorkian alone, but it doesn't bother him; he's gotten used to it.

Kevorkian is a man certain of everything. He describes himself as hyper-critical and cynical, but not cynical enough. He bridles at insincerity. Though he will lose his temper, he may feel terrible afterward, chiding himself saying, "I shouldn't have done that. Shouldn't have said that. Should have kept quiet."

Though a student of death, he is a lover of the classics and an artist of sorts. He is self-taught on the keyboard and also composes music; he has played the flute since high school. Kevorkian's musical taste is partial to Bach and Handel.

His "music room" is jury-rigged by placing an electronic keyboard organ like a bridge between one chair and a K-Mart end table; he selects one musical score from a stack of complicated choices. Instead of Carnegie Hall, he is sitting in an austere spare room playing baroque music in a run down apartment building. It's clean, it works, but it's spartan at best.

DR. DEATH

He doesn't eat much and has simple tastes in food: dry toast with a little jelly for breakfast; a can of corn plus a pear for lunch; perhaps, a grilled cheese sandwich -- with American cheese -- for dinner.

After police impounded his 1968 VW camper bus, Kevorkian rode around an old bicycle -- a hand-me-down from a sister -- 15 miles to medical seminars at William Beaumont Hospital. He exists on $537 a month in Social Security and some slight savings. He buys his clothes at the local Salvation Army Thrift Store.

In his sparsly furnished, gloomy living room rests a plywood desk. Kevorkian has converted a room of his apartment to an office suite as his views have made it difficult for him to find professional work. Jack's cardboard-box file cabinets were gleaned from the trash. He scribes his reports on a typewriter.

Kevorkian has no desire to be rich. Many have invited him on a speaking tour where, on the circuit, he could earn $10,000 per talk. He won't do it.

While Kevorkian has few friends, he does play poker about every fourth night or so. He doesn't smoke but says, "Once in a while, I like to chew on a cigar because it adds to the atmosphere, you know?"

KEVORKIAN HUMOR

Woody Allen swears that "There are only two topics worth talking about -- death and sex. And nobody wants to talk about death." But Kevorkian is the exception: "Everybody is afraid to even talk about these things," Kevorkian says, but "I am not afraid."

Blessed with a marvelous sense of humor, Kevorkian takes in stride the macabre amusement that some associate with *Dr. Death*. At Washington's Gridiron Club dinner, Senate Minority Leader Bob Dole was roasting George Bush who had just lost his presidential reelec-

12

tion bid, characterizing it as "Dr. Kevorkian's first effort as a campaign manager."

L.A. Daily News sports writer Mike Ventre, noting that Cleveland had signed quarterback Vinny Testaverde, bantered, "It's akin to finding one of the last doctors who makes house calls, but his name is Kevorkian."

Jay Leno can't seem to resist Kevorkian jokes, teasing that his suicide machine, the *Mercitron*, has "a snooze button for people who want to live 10 minutes longer."

A PARIAH TO SOME

A retired pathologist, Kevorkian worked at Pontiac General Hospital (1959-1966) and was Chief of Pathology at Detroit's Saratoga General Hospital (1970-1976). He moved to California and had a post at Beverly Hills Medical Center in Los Angeles, living out of his van for a while because cheap apartments were tough to find. He last worked at Pacific Hospital in Long Beach (1980-1981).

While he has never been fired, Kevorkian is a pariah to some. He has managed to alienate most of the powers-that-be; indeed he could not even secure work as a lowly emergency medical services technician at William Beaumont Hospital after retiring.

Kevorkian rails about the persecution of the Armenian people, saying, ". . .my forefathers . . . were gassed, Armenians were killed in every conceivable way. Pregnant women were split open with bayonets and babies taken out. They were drowned, burned, heads were smashed in vices. They were chopped in half."

When Kevorkian moved from California back to Michigan, he shipped his possessions: furniture, organ, harpsichord, books, oil paintings he created, many personal records. But Fate discarded these treasures. "It's awful," Kevorkian says, reminiscing of his immigrant Armenian parents who, under siege by the Turks, had also lost all of life's treasures.

Rock star Janis Joplin sang, "Freedom's just another word for -- nothin' left to lose." In harmony, Kevorkian lilts, "I have nothing to lose. Other doctors can't do what I do because they have responsibilities to people that I don't have and they have families and positions to protect."

His cramped, home-office allows him to set up an easel and paints. He studied oil painting about 30 years ago in a Pontiac, Michigan adult education night school class. While some claim that he paints in bizarre colors, the artist Kevorkian explains, "I don't like anything banal." The physician-artist would describe his paintings of death and abortion as surrealistic.

MEDICAL SCHOLAR

Jack Kevorkian, M.D. is an internationally-credited medical scholar having published nearly 30 papers in indexed journals on diverse topics including the ethics and practice of euthanasia; the marketing of human organs and tissue; and terminal human experimentation. He has written booklets: a brief history of the autopsy; medical aspects of capital punishment; a philosophical reflection on the mysteries of existence, life and death. In 1991, his book -- *Prescription Medicide: The Goodness of Planned Death* -- was published.

Some of his more esoteric writing would impress both physician and lay person alike:

1956 *The fundus oculi and the determination of death.*[11]

1959 *History of human dissection.*[12]

1961 *Transfusion of postmortem human blood.*[3]

1972 *Mercury content of human tissues during the 20th Century.*[14]

1973 *Leiomyosarcoma of large arteries and veins.*[15]

1984 *A coherent grid system of coordinates for precise anatomical localization.*[16]

Since 1986, however, Kevorkian has dedicated his efforts to the "long-range goal of terminal experimentation."

NO MORE "JUMPING OUT OF WINDOWS"

Kevorkian has observed that, as a "compassionately hypocritical society," we deny ". . .access to dignified, humane and extremely beneficial means [for suicide]. . . ." The result is that ". . .tormented lives continue to be ended by all kinds of makeshift, violent, messy and torturous methods. . . ." Electively, ". . .the practice of medicide is to offer an alternative to the inevitable violent methods now used by suffering patients to end their own lives." Toward that end, Kevorkian invented the Mercitron.

Kevorkian's homemade device is at least quick, painless and neat for some thirty thousand people who commit suicide each year in the United States, more than half do so by gunshot, usually with a handgun. Less popular methods include: hanging, strangulation and suffocation; gas and vapors; auto accidents and jumps; drugs, corrosives and caustics. The Mercitron was a more attractive alternative in any event.

Kevorkian's contraption, the Mercitron, offered the goodness of planned death to mere mortals who would accelerate their own passing. The Mercitron was like stealing death from the gods. It was death-on-command at the flick of a switch, peaceful and painless.

DR. DEATH

By 1989, Kevorkian's Mercitron was ready for patients. It sat in Kevorkian's spartan apartment, next to a few cardboard cartons and a broken black-and-white television set. The *Detroit Free Press* Magazine said, that with the Mercitron, you could. . .

> *Plug it into a wall socket, punch it into your arm, press a button and five minutes later, you're dead. It's painless, portable and legal. Kevorkian is certain it would work, if only someone would give it a whirl. Applications are being accepted.*

> *Oppressed by a fatal disease, a severe handicap, a crippling deformity? Show him proper, compelling medical evidence that you should die and Dr. Jack Kevorkian will help you kill yourself, free of charge.*[17]

Kevorkian said, "I don't care how it seems to healthy people. I'm here to help sick people."

Now, all that Kevorkian needed to inaugurate his new medical specialty of *obitiatry* was a volunteer. Obviously Kevorkian could not test his suicide machine on himself. Indeed, Kevorkian needed a first patient in this terminal experiment for the debut of his Mercitron.

While the cost of this medicide procedure might involve $80 to $200 in out-of-pocket expenses, Kevorkian never charges for his services, saying "I don't even charge for materials. To me, that's money well-spent." The few donations he has received from families of his medicide patients have been deposited into a special account for future research.

In coming years, Kevorkian would receive many inquiries about his Mercitron and his services as an obitiatrist.

chapter two
Last Syllable of Time

J anet Adkins and her husband, Ron, an investment broker, lived in Portland, Oregon. "She had a real *joie de vivre*, a real spirit for life. She climbed the 11,239-foot-high Mt. Hood in the Cascade Mountains near her home, she climbed the Himalayas," said Neil Adkins, one of Adkins' three sons. She taught English as a second language part-time at Portland Community College for 13 years. Her piano students came to this accomplished musician's home for lessons.

Ronald Adkins described his wife as vivacious, a gem, the kind of person who opened up new worlds for those who entered her life. Her tennis partner said she was strong and quick and she had a heart, not giving up. Her pastor at the First Unitarian church said she embraced life lovingly.

The Adkins' home was about 100 miles north of the national headquarters of The Hemlock Society USA, a right-to-die group based in Eugene, Oregon.

DR. DEATH

For some time, Adkins and husband Ron had been noticing the impairment of her memory; it was subtle and becoming gradually progressive. Abruptly and somewhat callously, her doctor announced on June 12, 1989, that Adkins was diagnosed as having Alzheimer disease, a degenerative brain malady that causes severe disorientation and, eventually, death. Though she was not then terminally ill, the horror of such a life was evident to Adkins, not to mention how tragic it would be for her husband.

This fearsome, horrible disease claims 100,000 victims annually. Adkins would become a victim of her deadly disease. Stress and strain, anxious days and sleepless nights; sometimes she would wander, other times fall. Sometimes only a little supervision, other times constant.

Alzheimer disease would take a terrible toll on Ron Adkins, her loyal husband, who would assume an immense responsibility, day in and day out, week after week, months on end. Over time, Ron Adkins would be fully responsible for his wife's nutrition. He would pay diligent attention to her personal hygiene and grooming. He would be her recreational director, struggling to offer his wife a restraint-free environment. Being his wife's helping hands would exhaust him physically and emotionally. On the easy days, it would still be hard. Over time, Ron would become so worn out that he could not function effectively and he would fall ill.

Over its course, Alzheimer disease would strip Adkins' memories, attack her thinking and finally crush her ability to function physically; the dreaded disease would attack her central nervous system, progressively impairing her memory and behavior. A *New York Times* reader describes the disease:

Dear Editor:

Alzheimer is an incurable, relentless destruction of the functioning mind.... ...For the victim, these [so-called "good" years] are the nightmare years, the time when each loss of competence is noted and the next one dreaded. Frustration, fear and anger chase one another in the continuous downward spiral.

By the time intelligent conversation has given way to singsong gibberish and limbs have forgotten their function, the opportunity to opt out is long since past.

It is only at the onset of the disease that the victim still retains some control over her fate. ...Some may wish to exit before their competence is gone and their image in the memories of others is diminished....

I would consider it a blessing if Dr. Kevorkian is around if and when I need him.

Yet, for Adkins and other Alzheimer sufferers, there was a ray of optimism -- any day could bring a cure. Nonetheless, the news of her diagnosis devastated her. Everything she cherished would be slowly stolen from her, piece by piece, until she had forgotten everyone and everything she loved and enjoyed. Adkins simply wanted to find the exit before she lost the person who she had become over the last half century. She would exercise the ultimate act of free will, a choice she insisted was her right.

19

Then age 54, Adkins was a mentally-competent victim of rapidly advancing Alzheimer disease. She was not yet physically or mentally destroyed by her disease. She appreciated that, in time, the entire burden of her disease would be carried by her husband and her family. It would be a back-breaking soul-destroying job, demanding round-the-clock presence, diapering, feeding, bathing.

Though death was stalking her, it had not yet arrived at the foot of her bed. But death would wait to steal her breath should she blink an eye. Inescapably, she was dying along with the life she had made for herself.

Upon hearing her diagnosis and at the very next instant, she decided to accelerate her death before she became too debilitated and while she was still alert. "If I do not stand up for myself," thought Adkins, "then who will be my advocate? And if not now, finally, then when?" Adkins wanted to keep the image of herself clean for her family and friends, not wanting to muddy it up with a lot of ugly business.

"I can . . . assure you that Mrs. Adkins had a longstanding, voluntary, well-considered philosophy of life that included her wanting the option of a physician's aid in case of terminal illness or a disease such as Alzheimer," wrote Myriam Coppens, the Adkins family therapist.

"It's not a matter of how long you live," husband Ron Adkins volunteered, "but the quality of life you live. It was Janet's life and her decision to chose."

CALLING DOCTOR DEATH

Reading *Newsweek*, on November 13, 1989, Ronald Adkins had learned about the Mercitron. In Oregon, assisted suicide is a crime. His wife's Alzheimer diagnosis had been pronounced earlier that year.

Had he lived in Michigan during June 1987, Ron Adkins might have seen Kevorkian's classified ad in the "Medical/Dental Counseling" section of a major Detroit newspaper:[19]

DEATH COUNSELING

IS SOMEONE IN YOUR FAMILY TERMINALLY ILL?

Does he or she wish to
die — and with dignity?

CALL PHYSICIAN CONSULTANT
{Telephone No.}

That ad was all but ignored. Nevertheless, more than two years later, Ronald Adkins telephoned Royal Oak, Michigan. "The world is looking at us," thought Ronald Adkins as he dialed the telephone.

Kevorkian well remembers that "Ron Adkins' rich, baritone, matter-of-fact voice was tinged with a bit of expectant anxiety as he calmly explained the tragic situation of his beloved wife."[20]

"The reality of death is more apparent to more people," Adkins explained as he pleaded with his wife to reconsider her decision and, perhaps, try the promising but developing drug, Tacrine® or THA, in a program at the University of Washington in Seattle. Kevorkian agreed saying, "I concurred that Janet should enroll in the program because any candidate for the Mercitron must have exhausted every potentially beneficial medical intervention, no matter how remotely promising."[21]

From December 1989 through March 1990, Janet participated in experimental treatment. During those

21

months, Janet embraced life again, fully realizing she had been granted the option of assisted-suicide. Giving a patient control over their final months, weeks, days liberates that patient to live those precious hours more fully.

Kevorkian has reflected that ". . .the mere knowledge of the availability, or just the anticipation of making use, of doctor-assisted suicide has a strangely salubrious effect on patients, as though adding zest to what little life remains."[22]

After some months, however, Janet's gusto was interrupted when researchers deemed the drug to be ineffective. As Adkins' condition worsened, she became more resolved to accelerate her death.

In April 1990, Ronald Adkins again telephoned Kevorkian after seeing the pathologist on national television with a prototype of his suicide machine, the Mercitron.

"I was obliged to scrutinize Janet's clinical records and to consult with her personal doctor," Kevorkian reports.[23]

Kevorkian insisted that Adkins be rational at the time of the assisted suicide. Her decision was well thought out. She was consistent in her desires and the plans she was making. She was a strong-willed person.

On May 18, Kevorkian telephoned Dr. Murray Raskind of the University of Washington Medical Center in Seattle; Dr. Raskind was Adkins' attending physician.

Kevorkian recalls an uncooperative attitude by the physicians who opposed her plan to resign from life. Her choice to die was difficult to respect because she was in the earliest stages of Alzheimer disease. Dr. Raskind warned Kevorkian: "It is totally inappropriate of you, Dr. Kevorkian, to assist in Janet's suicide because she has several more years of an enjoyable life." Adkins' doctor contended she would remain mentally competent for at least another year with time to enjoy many pleasures.[24]

"She dreaded what would have come. I would too," said Kevorkian. "I don't want to die of Alzheimer -- smeared with your own urine and feces, don't know who you are. Come on!"

While Kevorkian made no formal diagnosis, as the obitiatrist he reviewed her medical records which confirmed her husband Ron's report of progressive mental failure. Obitiatrist Kevorkian obtained two medical opinions and Adkins' medical records from two treating physicians, all confirming her condition. Though she was not imminently terminal at that time, it was clear to Kevorkian that the experimental treatment had failed to improve her condition.

Kevorkian assessed his conversations with her husband. "From Ron's narrative, I concluded that her doctor's opinion was wrong and that time was of the essence. Because Janet's condition was deteriorating and there was nothing else to arrest it, I decided to accept her as the first candidate -- a qualified, justifiable candidate if not *ideal* -- being well aware of my vulnerability to criticism of picayune and overly emotional critics."[25]

Criticized for having assisted Adkins after a short personal acquaintance of only two days, Kevorkian defends: "Because of shameful stonewalling by her own doctors, Janet was forced to refer herself to me."[26]

Kevorkian accepted Adkins as the first patient for his prescription: medicide! "I agree to help you . . . in the spirit of rationality which you are about to lose," Kevorkian told her. "The highest ethical principle to me is individual self-determination," Kevorkian advised.

While Adkins' decision to use the Mercitron was bound to be controversial, her family did not realize to what extent. In pursuit of death with dignity, Janet sought Kevorkian's aid-in-dying; she sought a physician's assistance to effectuate her own mercy killing, as there was no legalized euthanasia.

THE NECESSARY PAPERS

Two days before she planned to die, on Saturday, June 2, 1990, Adkins flew into Detroit Metropolitan Airport from Oregon. She made this 2,000 trip for one purpose. To die. In her entourage were husband Ronald and her close friend, Carroll Rehmke. These sojourners stayed at a motel in Romulus, Michigan near the airport.

That Saturday afternoon, Kevorkian arrived at their motel accompanied by his sisters, Margo Janus and Flora Holzheimer; Holzheimer had traveled from Frankfurt, Germany to be with her brother. After a few minutes of small talk, the purpose of Adkins' trip was discussed.

For the next 45 minutes or so, with Holzheimer videotaping the interview, Kevorkian attended to some of the necessary details: "I had already prepared authorization forms signifying Janet's intent, determination and freedom of choice, which she readily agreed to sign,"[27] Kevorkian detailed. He then cross-examined his patient:

Kevorkian: Now, Janet, do you want to go on?

Adkins: No, I don't.

Kevorkian: Not at all?

Adkins: No. I see my life ending. I know that I will end up in a nursing home confined to bed, tied down, not knowing who I am, what I am, or where I am. . . . I wish to end it now while I'm cognizant.

Ronald Adkins said, "I'm for it because she wants it, because I love her. She should have the right not to suffer and should have a humane way to exit."

"Now you don't want her to go on?" Kevorkian queried Ron Adkins.

"No, I don't."

Then Kevorkian turned to Adkins. He continued to assess her candidacy. The doctor asked:

Q. You know what you're asking me to do? You realize that?

A. Yes.

Q. You want help from me?

A. I do.

Q. You realize that I can make arrangements for everything but *you* would have to do it? *You* would have to push the button?

A. I understand.

Q. Though you realize that you can stop anytime?

A. I know.

Q. You don't *have* to go on.

A. Right.

Q. But what does that mean to you?

A. It means that's the end of my life.

Q. What's the word for the end of life, what is it when you stop living?

A. It means . . . you're dead.

Q. Some say you're doing the wrong thing. What would you tell them?

A. I want out.

Repeatedly during the nearly hour-long videotaped interview, Kevorkian noted that Adkins' memory had failed her badly. Had he waited four to six months longer, she would have been too incompetent mentally to qualify as a candidate for the Mercitron.

"Here again, while she was resolute in her decision and absolutely mentally competent, her impaired memory was apparent," Kevorkian records. "At this time, Ron and Carroll also signed a statement attesting to Janet's mental competence."[28]

HER LAST SUPPER

That same Saturday evening around 5:30 p.m., this coterie of six went to a Madison Heights, Michigan restaurant to share a dinner together which lasted until after midnight. Kevorkian's purpose was less to sup than to observe his patient. Adkins seemed to be among those able to rationally end their own lives.

Kevorkian watched Adkins that evening over dinner saying, "I constantly observed Janet's behavior and assessed her moods as well as the content and quality of her thoughts. There was absolutely no doubt that her mentality was intact and that she was not the least depressed over her impending death."[29]

While Adkins would laugh appropriately, indicating

26

clear and coherent comprehension, she was increasingly embarrassed and uneasy at forgetting the various current topics of discussion that evening. Shortly past midnight, on Sunday morning, the dinner group adjourned.

Ron and Janet enjoyed their last full day together and alone on Sunday. They strolled together along the St. Clair River in Port Huron, Michigan.

FAREWELL NOTE

On Monday, June 4, the morning of her death, Adkins rose early. She composed a note:

To whom it may concern:

I have decided for the following reason to take my own life. This is a decision taken in a normal state of mind and is fully considered.

I have Alzheimer disease and do not want to let it progress any further. I don't choose to put my family or myself through the agony of this terrible disease.

Janet E. Adkins

Adkins signed and dated her note, indicating that she wanted her eyes donated for cornea research. Her note was witnessed by her husband, Ronald, and her friend, Rehmke.

When Kevorkian's sisters arrived to fetch Adkins from the motel, she tendered her suicide note to Holzheimer. Tearfully, Janet exchanged farewells with her husband and Rehmke, both grieving terribly. Per Adkins' wish, both were to stay behind.

Rehmke too had crafted a farewell message for Adkins. She handed her note to Holzheimer, asking that it be read before Adkins was to press the switch on the Mercitron.

NO VACANCY

Before Adkins traveled from Portland to the Detroit airport, Kevorkian had been diligently searching for a suitable site. Discussing his candor, Kevorkian narrated, "I always explained that I planned to assist a suffering patient to commit suicide. I soon found how difficult a matter it could be."

Being forthright about his intentions and despite so-called "sympathetic supporters," Kevorkian was repeatedly denied the use of countless motels, funeral homes, churches, rental buildings, clinics, and physician's offices. "Dr. Kevorkian even inquired about using one of our EMS vehicles before Janet Adkins committed suicide," said Jon Eschbach, Jr. an owner of Fleet Ambulance Company. "At the time, we couldn't cooperate."

Kevorkian reflected that, "Most dismaying yet was the refusal of people who are known supporters and active campaigners for euthanasia to allow Janet and me the use of their homes."[30]

Kevorkian refused to be secretive about his plans. "I acted openly, ethically, legally and with complete and uncompromising honesty."[31] Yet, Kevorkian was shunned at every turn.

"I had made a Herculean effort to provide a desirable, clinical setting. Literally and sadly, there was *no room at the inn.* Now, having been refused everywhere I applied, the *only alternative* remaining was my 1968 camper and a suitable campground," Kevorkian apologized.[32] Among his minimal requirements was an electrical outlet to service the Mercitron.

VALLEY OF DEATH

The elected site of this epochal event was in the remote Groveland Oaks Park, near Holly, Michigan. The park was pleasant and idyllic.

Though the white VW bus was 22 years old and corroded on the outside, the interior was clean, orderly and comfortable. In gloomy contrast, the weather was damp.

The VW camper sat dutifully in its rented slip, its sliding side door rolled open. There was a built-in bed, covered with freshly laundered sheets and a clean pillow. For the occasion, new draperies shrouded the windows.

Kevorkian, self-sufficient as always, drove himself in the VW to the site of this makeshift "clinic" at Groveland Park arriving at about 8:30 a.m. on this cloudy Monday morning. Inventor Kevorkian was visibly nervous and fidgety setting up the Mercitron. Kevorkian spent the next hour giving his makeshift suicide machine a few test runs.

About 9:30 a.m., Kevorkian's sisters and Adkins arrived. At one point, Kevorkian had turned to reach for some pliers and, in the cramped confines of the VW camper, he inadvertently bumped the container of thiopental -- the solution which would carry Adkins into an irreversible, surgical depth sleep. Distraught, Kevorkian watched helplessly as more than half of the container spilled.

Dismayed at this frightful accident, the foursome piled into a car and drove for the next two and one-half hours back to Kevorkian's Royal Oak apartment on another round trip to replenish the anesthesia. Kevorkian reflected, "I was fairly sure the unspilled remainder was enough to induce and maintain adequate unconsciousness. Nonetheless, I chose not to take the risk," the doctor confides. I drove the 45 miles home and got some more."[33]

About 12 Noon, the entourage returned to the park. Adkins remained in the car with Kevorkian's sister, Janus, while his other sister, Holzheimer, assisted her brother with final preparations. Holzheimer was so proud of her brother. "He is a genius," she thought.

For the next two hours, Adkins was calm but impatient to get on with the procedure while Kevorkian was rigging up the Mercitron and retesting it. The procedure was further delayed due to a mechanical difficulty with the apparatus. However, by 2:00 p.m. everything was finally all prepared for Janet's final trip.

Adkins was then summoned through the VW bus sliding side door, as if being beckoned to approach the back Gates of Heaven. "I feel sorry for having to do this with Janet," Kevorkian said to himself. "I have empathy and pity for her. It's one thing to talk about it . . . but it's totally different when it comes down to doing it." Kevorkian was incredulous, surprising himself at how emotional he felt.

Silently Adkins laid down, fully clothed on the VW bus camper bed. Kevorkian describes the details, "I cut small holes in her nylon stockings at the ankles, attached ECG electrodes to her ankles and wrists and covered her body with a light blanket."[34] Holzheimer retrieved the note, written earlier that morning by Adkins' friend, Carroll Rehmke, and read the following message aloud:

My dear Friend,

My heart weeps for you and for all of us. Keeping this vigil, watching you say goodbye over and over to those you love will change my life forever. My knees shake, my being

*feels broken and I don't know how to say
goodbye ... except to just say, goodbye my
friend.*

*Shalom, Janet. You leave us with love. Peace
to you. I will miss you and there are no
words to tell you how very much. You have
helped make my life richer. You are leaving
us with courage. I am in awe, in pain.*

I love you,

Carroll

Then there was a reading of the Lord's Prayer.
Holzheimer read the Twenty-Third Psalm: "Yea, though
I walk through the valley of the shadow of death, I will
fear no evil: for Thou are with me."

Adkins calmly listened as Kevorkian, wearing a
wrinkled, white golf hat, carefully reinstructed her on
operating the Mercitron. Adkins would take her own
life by pressing a button on Kevorkian's homemade suicide machine, the Mercitron, which would inject her
with lethal drugs.

The Mercitron worked like an IV, introducing into
the veins pentothal, a fast-acting barbiturate that produces almost instantaneous unconsciousness after a
single dose. Moments after slipping into a deep sleep,
a high-level of potassium chloride rushes into the veins,
paralyzing the heart muscle like a heart attack and shut-
ting down the respiratory system completely. The
Mercitron offered a painless and merciful death in minutes.

Kevorkian used a syringe with a large needle to en-
sure a heavy flow of the drugs intended to kill. But
Adkins had fragile veins. Kevorkian failed at least twice

to successfully insert the needle. Her vein was elusive. All the while, Adkins was silent and very, very calm.

Perhaps, Kevorkian was nervous; perhaps, Adkins' veins were fragile. In time, Kevorkian was able to locate and pierce a vein on her right arm. He started a harmless saline solution through the IV.

The last moments of Adkins' visit to this Earth were peaceful and loving. Kevorkian removed the safety cap from the button that would release the drugs. He turned on the ECG and indicated to Adkins that all was ready by saying, "Now."

Adkins quickly hit the switch of the Mercitron three times with the outer edge of her palm. Ten seconds later, her eyelids began to droop, but she gazed at Doctor Death, reaching up as if she wanted to kiss him. He bent over to hear her whisper, "Thank you, thank you."

"Have a nice trip," Kevorkian replied as her eyelids closed.

Adkins was unconscious and absolutely still for several minutes. Then, she coughed twice. Kevorkian became concerned that the drug flow was interrupted. He picked up one of the bottles containing the solution and shook it. He asked himself, "Is she really dying?"

Kevorkian was aghast and admitted, "I was scared because she was my first patient. She had a very strong heart. She got a whopping dose of potassium chloride and her heart was still beating. But it failed. . . . I was relieved, not because she died, but because it turned out successfully for her," the obitiatrist sighed.

Kevorkian knew that he would have finished Adkins off himself if anything had gone wrong with the suicide machine. "I would break the law and finish it myself," Kevorkian had pledged to himself.

Most importantly, Kevorkian said, "I remained in personal attendance during the second most meaningful medical event in Adkins' earthly existence. Were

Hippocrates alive today, it's not hard to guess what he would say about all this."[35]

Six minutes after she alone had activated the Mercitron, Adkins died peacefully. The ECG confirmed this but, to be sure, Kevorkian examined Adkins' eyes which indicated cessation of blood flow and, therefore, cessation of flow to the brain and, obviously, cessation of flow to all organs -- or practical death.

"It was 2:30 p.m.," Kevorkian later wrote, "suddenly -- for the first time that cold, dank day -- warm sunshine bathed the park."[36]

POLICE ARRIVE

Kevorkian called police who, in turn, impounded the van and the suicide machine. The nearly hour-long videotape was seized in a court-authorized search of Kevorkian's Royal Oak apartment.

"He's an irresponsible doctor . . . it was an undignified death," proclaimed Assistant Prosecuting Attorney Michael Modelski. "We need to find out what happened in Groveland Oaks."

Hulp biz zelfdoding . . . help with suicide, the Dutch call it. For nearly two decades now, Holland refuses to convict doctors who practice assisted-suicide upon the specific plea of their patient.

This was the first time Kevorkian publicly acknowledged his participation in physician-assisted suicide, or what he terms *medicide.* Kevorkian was fighting for a cause for which he is willing to go to jail -- the right of a person who is terminally ill or suffering terribly to take their life.

But Kevorkian said he wasn't worried about jail. "Assisting a suicide is not illegal in Michigan, so I doubt I'll go to jail, but if I do, then that's all right. Let them make me a martyr," the doctor challenged.

DR. DEATH

"I'm not saying you should kill patients or shouldn't kill patients. But it should be a medical service, like it is in Holland where they have 8,000 to 10,000 euthanasias a year," Kevorkian declared. "Michigan leads the country and the civilized world -- outside of the Netherlands," where physician-assisted suicide is not prosecuted, Kevorkian said.

"If the patient wants to die, it is a right. Personal autonomy is the highest right," Kevorkian declared. But about the prosecutor, Kevorkian surmised, "My hunch is . . . he's going to bring charges."

MARTYRDOM BEGINS

One potential supporter of Kevorkian was quoted as saying, "This man is beautiful beyond mortal words. To put himself out there, to sacrifice himself like that . . . God bless him."

But Dr. Death's trials were now to begin. "Unfortunately for our own and succeeding generations," Kevorkian lamented, "there is no comparably superior extrinsic human entity to cut short the tragic martyrdom of today's hapless heretics who dare openly to denounce and disobey the patently immoral laws of a now worldwide social coalition prohibiting even stringently controlled planned death."

Ronald Adkins and Carroll Rehmke had spent the day worried and concerned. Finally, near 3:00 p.m., Kevorkian telephoned Ronald Adkins to report that Janet Adkins had ended her life.

"After Dr. Kevorkian called me, I immediately went from the motel to the funeral parlor," said Adkins who had made arrangements for his wife's body to be cremated after an autopsy by the Oakland County Medical Examiner.

After returning his rental car at the airport, Adkins headed for the airline departure gate, intending to leave for Portland, Oregon. Adkins' departure did not go as smoothly as planned.

"I felt it was a very hectic and traumatic day and I had already had as much as I could handle," said Adkins who wanted to avoid questioning by Michigan State Police that Monday afternoon.

At Detroit Metropolitan Airport, Adkins first sought to evade state police attempts to identify him while he boarded his commercial flight. Suspicious, the officer phoned in for more information about the woman's suicide, the facts of which were still unfolding. Adkins refused to accompany the officer to a telephone to speak with investigators about his wife's medicide, boarding the plane instead. Then, a state police detective temporarily halted Adkins' departure, ordering the airplane not to depart from the gate, forcing Adkins to deplane. Adkins was allowed to leave Michigan only after he acknowledged his identity and stated he knew about the incident.

INTERNATIONAL PUBLICITY

Janet Adkins' departure from this Earth gained international attention, capturing the nation's interest from Maine to California. The news reports of Adkins' death spread far and wide, accented by the Mercitron, a home-made suicide machine designed by Jack Kevorkian, M.D. Adkins self-deliverance made the cover of *Time* magazine, was reported on by *The New York Times* and Kevorkian was an invited guest on *Geraldo*.

But Kevorkian was not charged with any crime -- until a good six months later.

KEVORKIAN CHARGED WITH MURDER

"Suicide is not a crime in the state of Michigan," said Oakland County Prosecutor Richard Thompson. But "it's a dangerous silent message, an attitude that prevailed in Nazi Germany," he warned. Unlike dozens of states, there was no statutory law in Michigan against assisted suicide. But Prosecutor Thompson left open the possibility that he might press murder charges against Kevorkian. Like Kevorkian, Prosecutor Thompson is also of Armenian heritage.

Not until six months after Adkins died was Kevorkian charged with first degree murder in her death. The murder charges came down on December 3, 1990.

The headstrong doctor initiated quite a ruckus outside a circuit court judge's private office in the Oakland County courthouse before one court hearing. Kevorkian demanded that state police put the handcuffs on him. "It's a charade. Let's make the charade right to the letter. . . . I want the cuffs. I want the cuffs," Kevorkian insisted to Detective Sergeant David Haire.

Later, despite his insistence, Kevorkian was taken into custody without handcuffs and arraigned in Michigan's 52nd District Court. He was held on $50,000 cash bond, required to pay $5,000 or 10 percent of the bond to be released. Kevorkian spent several hours in jail before posting bond. The penalty for first degree murder in Michigan is life in prison without parole.

Thompson said Kevorkian was charged because, although Adkins pushed the button starting the flow of the medication that killed her, it was Kevorkian who gave her the drugs, injected the needle allowing the drugs to flow and advised her how to operate the Mercitron -- all for the sole purpose of killing her.

"Dr. Kevorkian was the primary and legal cause of Janet Adkins' death," Prosecutor Thompson declared. "He cannot avoid his criminal culpability *by the clever use of a switch*."

Thompson sounded the alarm that Michigan may become the suicide mecca of the nation. But Kevorkian was disdainful, "I don't take this seriously. This is all immoral anyway. . . . What happens to me is immaterial. The time has come for physician-assisted suicide." In his own mind, Kevorkian had no trouble sorting out "the conflict between what one *wants* to do and what one *ought* to do."[37]

But one writer to the editor of *The Advisor Newspaper* was more caustic and disparaging, writing:[38]

Dear Editor:

Physician-assisted suicide will never fly in this country.

The American Medical Association isn't interested in providing a dignified and inexpensive way to end life, as long as doctors can continue to drag out a death and empty out the pockets of not only the patient, but those of his family as well.

CRIMINAL CHARGES DISMISSED

In December 1990, at his preliminary examination, the court heard evidence to determine whether there was probable cause to believe that a crime had been committed and, if so, whether there was probable cause to believe that Kevorkian was the one who committed that crime.

Dr. Jacob Chason, neuropathologist affiliated with Wayne State University Medical School examined Adkins' brain tissue after her death. He indicated she had a severe case of Alzheimer disease.

Normally, about eight or so senile plaques can usually be found in each microscope slide specimen taken from a healthy person of Adkins' age. However, the number of plaques found in Adkins' tissue specimens were uncountable," Dr. Chason testified. "The number of plaques I saw in this patient was greater than any I have ever seen in other Alzheimer patients."

Nonetheless, Assistant Prosecutor Modelski did not hesitate to accuse Kevorkian of intending to kill Adkins. "Liar! Liar!," Kevorkian's sister, Janus, hissed at the prosecutor from the back of the courtroom, causing a brief stir. Janus believed otherwise, for she had waited outside her brother's VW van while Adkins activated the Mercitron.

However, after all of the evidence was received, 52nd District Judge Gerald McNally in Clarkston, Michigan threw out the murder charges against Kevorkian, citing the 1983 *Campbell* ruling by the Michigan Court of Appeals.

Judge McNally hoped his decision would be challenged. "I certainly hope it doesn't end with my decision," Judge McNally said. Prosecutor Thompson obliged him and appealed.

District Judge McNally also noted, "The legislature has a responsibility and I would hope they would step out and meet it." The judge said, "Without legislation, doctors will continue to tell patients -- *'Take two a day only, because more will kill you.'* -- knowing that patients will take matters into their own hands."

"I'd like to see a law that makes assisted suicide a choice," said Ronald Adkins. "It's an issue whose time has come and it's time we handled the issue. A law is needed that could protect our choice and protect the doctors who would be there to help us."

"I have faith we can create laws with checks and balances," Adkins prayed. "Religion is lagging, the law is lagging, medicine is lagging. The issue of medicide is here. You can't put it back in the box."

Pleased with the dismissal of the charges, Kevorkian grinned, "This is it . . . it's what I wanted," as well-wishers showered him with congratulations.

Yet Kevorkian insisted that the use of the Mercitron was in limbo until the legal status of assisted suicide becomes clearer. "I'm going to work with the authorities and within the system. I'm not going to break laws," Kevorkian pledged.

The very next day after Judge McNally dismissed the criminal charges against Kevorkian in the death of Adkins, the U.S. Supreme Court issued its first ruling on the thorny request to discontinue artificial life support, which would inevitably result in the death of Nancy Cruzan. Months earlier, Janet Adkins had decided that her life was soon to become, in her own mind, worthless. Supreme Court Justice Scalia commiserated:

> . . .The point at which life becomes worthless and the point at which the means necessary to preserve it become extraordinary or inappropriate, are neither set forth in the Constitution nor known to the nine Justices of [the United States Supreme] Court any better than they are known to nine people picked at random from the Kansas City telephone directory.[39]

Yet, Prosecutor Thompson was not content to permit Adkins to have judged when her own life became worthless or to allow Dr. Death to have accelerated her demise.

"Society is making me *Dr. Death,*" Kevorkian once grumbled. "Why can't they see? I'm *Dr. Life!*"

Instead, Prosecutor Thompson appealed judge McNally's dismissal of criminal charges against Kevorkian. And the wheels of justice did grind on.

DR. DEATH

CIVIL INJUNCTION GRANTED

In a separate civil proceeding, Oakland County Circuit Judge Alice Gilbert initially refused to grant prosecutors their request for a temporary order restraining Kevorkian from assisting in patient suicides. However, she did allow The Hemlock Society USA to participate in the case as a silent intervenor.

Accused by prosecutors of providing a tawdry death for Adkins with a "Keystone Kops" approach, Kevorkian acted as his own attorney at a two and one-half hour hearing.

But there was no law in Michigan prohibiting physician-assisted suicide. Kevorkian had defended himself before, saying ". . .It is wrong for . . . society to even try to judge the morality of an individual's action, deemed by that society to be immoral, when the individual concerned disagrees and performs the action in such a manner as not to infringe the autonomy of others or society's official rules of culpability."[40]

While Kevorkian said that medically assisted suicide is not an accepted practice in the medical profession, he argued it was needed in a world of rising suicide rates.

But one reviewer observed about Kevorkian's proposal for medicide that ". . .the idea's complete rationality is perhaps its greatest weakness."[41]

Two months after the murder charge against Kevorkian involving Adkins was dismissed, Judge Gilbert was not impressed. The judge issued an injunctive order, covering the entire state of Michigan. "He is causing death through unnatural means and nothing is more permanent than death," the judge announced.

"I'm out of business," Kevorkian vowed after Judge Gilbert issued an injunction . . . prohibiting Kevorkian from assisting in a patient's suicide. "It's the end of Dr. K. helping patients die." Or so Kevorkian alleged . . . out loud and in public.

40

Notwithstanding this statement, Kevorkian continued to correspond with those in need. Dr. Gary Sloan, a Vermont dentist who wished to end his life, asked Kevorkian about the Mercitron. Kevorkian obliged and corresponded to Dr. Sloan on July 10, 1990:

Dear Dr. Sloan:

The enclosed diagram will give you a general idea of how my device is constructed. There are several ways that details of the internal structure can be worked out satisfactorily. All it takes are a couple of solenoids and switches, a timer, and a couple of small valves (the latter can be those tiny plastic slides that come with the tubing on an I.V. sets). I'm sure you could put it all together yourself, especially if helped by a friend who is good with his hands or is an engineer. As you told me, you yourself could obtain the drugs.

Another option might be to make arrangements to come to Michigan if and when the court injunction against me is lifted. It is preferable to do the procedure in a private home or office of a friend or relative of yours who lives in Michigan (if that is possible and can be arranged). In all likelihood there will be some action on the injunction in 4-6 weeks at most, which you should hear about through news reports. If it is lifted, and if you are still interested, I could notify you so that you could begin making necessary arrangements.

Best wishes, Jack Kevorkian, M.D.

DR. DEATH

COURT OF PUBLIC OPINION

Kevorkian complained he is being hounded by an overzealous legal system and a hypocritical medical profession. "The courts would love to burn me at the stake and the prosecutor is trying to light the fire."

His attorney, Geoffrey Fieger, was more vivid, branding the authorities who were pursuing Kevorkian as "truly malevolent, sick people, acting like some kind of Terminator cops."

At one point, Fieger characterized Alice Gilbert as "incredibly stupid" and the laziest judge on the Oakland County Circuit Court. But Gilbert's rejoinder was, "I stand on my record."

"The law and ethics flatly don't mean a thing to me when a patient is in front of me and needs help," Kevorkian asserted. Yet, Kevorkian reluctantly agreed to voluntarily comply with a court order to get out of the suicide business.

BRASH AND BOLD

Kevorkian had read about attorney Fieger before retaining his services; the obitiatrist sorely needed a legal advocate. Fieger's one-page biography indicates no hobbies "other than kicking the bejesus out of opponents in court." Kevorkian is quick to come to the defense of his counsel, calling him brilliant:

It may look like confrontation, but when . . . you're dead right and your opponent is dead wrong, there can't be any compromise.

I might very well have been in jail without his pugnacity, his obstinance. If it's not a forceful man fighting, prosecutors very well could

42

*bulldoze over and put me in jail. You can't
bulldoze over Fieger; everyone knows that.*

*He may look like he's out of control but he's
not. I was like everybody at first. I didn't
see his full spectrum of behavior and his personal reactions and attitudes. As these unfolded, I learned never to second-guess him.*

Once, attorney Fieger ordered Kevorkian to cancel a
long-planned lecture at the national convention of the
American College of Forensic Psychiatry. The pathologist had been scheduled to address more than 200 pro-
fessionals on "Personal Autonomy in Physician-Assisted
Suicide." But at the 11th hour, Kevorkian could only
offer regrets saying, "I'm sorry, I can't make it. My lawyer won't let me because he's afraid I might say something that will incriminate me."

While client Jack Kevorkian has never disclosed what,
if anything, he has paid for Fieger's legal representation,
his attorney has confessed that "defending Kevorkian has
cost me money." Yet, Fieger readily admits, defending
Dr. Death has "made me famous. Everybody knows who
I am."

Fieger will concede that Kevorkian is not the best
public relations spokesperson on the issue of physician-
assisted suicide. Others, like Macomb County, Michigan
Prosecutor Carl Marlinga, don't dispute that analysis and
will go further, saying: "Dr. Kevorkian himself is a very
abrasive personality who is so convinced of his righ-
teousness that he tends to belittle anybody who disagrees with him." And when you mix Fieger's lawyering
". . .with Dr. Kevorkian's personality, it tends to obscure
some of the philosophical merits of their position,"
Marlinga remarked.

In turn, Fieger dismisses out of hand those who rebuke him: "Those so called critics, I laugh. Some people I think are jealous. Others are liars and they don't support Kevorkian and are mad. . .," Fieger sneers disparagingly. "By the way, this is just me," Fieger offers. "If someone doesn't like me, that's just tough."

Michigan's Health Services Bureau began an investigation of Kevorkian, also licensed in California where assisting a suicide is illegal. Kevorkian would face discipline by the state medical board and lose his license to practice *medicide*.

A PIONEER'S LAST REQUEST

Before Adkins traveled to Michigan to die, she had planned her hour-long funeral to be a joyous occasion. A string quartet played a selection of her favorite music. Pastor Alan Deale led the congregation in singing Beethoven's "Ode to Joy."

"Janet loved life, but she didn't fear death," said Judy Humison, one of three friends who spoke at her wake.

Another friend, Carroll Rehmke, who had accompanied her to Michigan, observed that Adkins "always judged people by their inner spirit. When she realized that the disease would destroy not only her body but, also, her spirit within, she made a decision." "She lived the life of a pioneer and that is exactly how she died," Carroll told about 300 people who attended her memorial service.

Adkins had one, last request which she entrusted to Kevorkian before she flicked the switch of the Mercitron. "Please publicize my case," she pleaded.

Appropriately, Janet Adkins made the cover of *Time* that week which carried *both* the news of her suicide -- plus news of a promising new treatment for Alzheimer sufferers.

44

chapter three
'Til Death Do Us Part

At their mobile home in Loomis, California -- near Sacramento and some 2,000 miles away from the remote county park where Janet Adkins traveled to commit suicide in 1990 -- Virginia and Bertram Harper heard the news. Janet Adkins' assisted suicide offered a ray of hope for Virginia Harper who was known as Ginger to friends and family. Ginger was 69 years old. Bertram Harper, known as Bob, was 72.

"The couple flew to Michigan," said Derek Humphry, executive director of The Hemlock Society USA, "because news reports about Dr. Jack Kevorkian and his Mercitron led them to believe that assisted suicide was legal in Michigan." After the couple read about Michigan's law in an article by The Hemlock Society USA, they had the mistaken impression that Michigan was among states that had no law against assisted suicide.

For several months after Adkins' death, Michigan had earned a short-lived reputation as the suicide mecca of the nation. True: Michigan had no statute outlawing suicide, nor did it have any law against assisted suicide; but that did *not* mean that Michigan had actually legalized assisted suicides.

The subtlety of all of these legalities, quite understandably, had escaped the Harpers. Besides, as their story was unfolding, Kevorkian was still a free man. Indeed, for a full six months after Janet Adkins' assisted suicide, the prosecutor had let sleeping dogs lie, bringing no charges against Kevorkian.

This is what the Harpers missed in August 1990: conflicting legal precedents made it unclear whether assisted suicide was then a crime in Michigan. Indeed, Michigan was not extending a welcoming hand to candidates wishing for assisted suicide.

HAPPY HOME

In the gravel driveway near the Harpers' double-wide manufactured home in the Glen Brook Mobile Home park sat the car of Ginger Harper's daughter, Shanda McGrew. The vehicle was covered by a form-fitting tarpaulin.

Topped with wood shingles and surrounded by white ceramic ducks, the Harpers had one of the most attractive places in this 160-home retirement community, surrounded by well-manicured shrubs and flower gardens. For more than 15 years, the Harpers' mobile home had rested in the rolling, oak-studded foothills of the Sierra Nevada mountains, 30 miles east of Sacramento. Front porch chimes beckoned visitors.

About a week before flying to Michigan, the Harpers could be seen in the mobile home park pool, splashing about like a couple of love-sick kids. A dozen neighbors would agree: Bob and Ginger Harper were about as nice as people get.

Ginger Harper had been a retired newspaper editor. Harper had the best pair of ears around, sympathetic ears for listening. A cheerful friend to entertain your problems or just plain talk.

Bob Harper retired in 1983 as a chemical engineer who had served with Dow Chemical, Union Carbide and the California Solid Waste Management Board. He was an MIT grad. It was service with a smile when a neighbor needed a TV, computer, or screen door fixed. And he always had a wry joke to tell. He volunteered his time as a driving instructor for retirees and as a tour guide at the nearby dam's historic power station.

Private people, the Harpers. Friends never quite knew where they were from, knew little of their children and less of their previous marriages. Ginger Harper had told no one that she had been a cancer patient, having lumps removed from her breasts twice. Some things you just kept to yourself.

And despite the joy she shared with her husband, Ginger had trouble walking. Though 72 years old, Bob would half-carry Ginger around from their trailer to the park pool where she could exercise her legs.

MEETING THROUGH A COMPANION AD

Bob Harper recalls fondly how he met Ginger back in the mid-sixties through a companion ad in *Fact* magazine. Harper had been very daring as she advertised:

WOMAN SEEKS MAN

A lot of woman seeks a loving man: Southern California divorcee / age, hips, bust . . .
— **all 45!** —

After a long-distance relationship, they married in 1967 and were together for 23 years.

CANCER ATTACKS

In 1983, Harper discovered a lump in her breast, but she refused to have a mastectomy. Though she chose less radical surgery and the lump was removed, the cancer had not been rooted out.

In 1989, another tumor appeared and it too was removed. Despite these surgeries, Harper was diagnosed as terminal.

Harper vividly remembered nursing a younger brother as he suffered and ultimately died from leukemia.

She had also watched a close friend die from lung cancer after extended chemotherapy and radiation. "My friend was in agony when she died. She had lost all dignity in her life; in the end, there was no quality left in her life," Harper observed. "If we don't have quality of life, then life is not worth living." Harper would rather commit suicide than suffer and lose dignity.

The couple had friends who had died very painful, lingering deaths. "We've seen friends die deaths that you would not put a dog through," Bob Harper recalled. "If you did, you'd land in jail."

FAILED SUICIDE ATTEMPT

In 1989, Harper had attempted suicide after learning that cancer had invaded her liver and possibly her spine.

"It happened very suddenly while I was away," her husband told authorities in a statement. "I came home and there was a message from a friend to meet Ginger at a Holiday Inn in Sacramento." When Bob inquired after his wife at the front desk, he was sent to a room she had rented.

The key was in the door. Bob found his wife alone, sitting on the floor, unconscious, slumped against a wall. Harper had taken sleeping pills and drank coffee liqueur. However, she passed out before being able to fasten a plastic bag around her neck.

When Harper was revived, she told her husband that she wanted him there if she tried suicide again. They agreed that each would rather commit suicide than face painful deaths and neither wanted to be kept alive by machines. With that in mind, the couple made a pact together: Bob would help his wife end her life . . . when *she* chose. Bob felt he had no choice but to honor her wish.

PILGRIMAGE TO MECCA

By 1990, Ginger Harper's breast cancer had metastasized to her liver. "The doctor gave Ginny from two months to two years to live," recalls her husband. It was then Ginger Harper began getting her affairs in order; Bob began preparing himself emotionally to help.

"I think she might have hung on a little longer if she had known her doctor could have helped her and if the doctor had been able to keep her reasonably pain-free," reflected McGrew, age 40. Kevorkian similarly noted, "Rather than increasing the incidence of suicide, the practice of medicide will reduce it substantially and at the same time immeasurably enhance human welfare."

When Harper awoke on August 17 in excruciating pain, she realized that she was in for a bad time. She announced that now was the time; she had made her decision to fly to Michigan." She was determined not to suffer a slow, painful death from liver cancer.

Yet, her home state of California is one of some two dozen states where assisted suicide is a specific crime. At that time, the Harpers mistakenly understood that

Michigan was the only state where assisted suicide was "clearly" legal.

On August 18, 1990, less than three months after Janet Adkins had made her final exit, Bob and Ginger Harper flew to Detroit Metropolitan Airport. Besides the mistaken belief that assisted suicide was legal in Michigan, they also carried a note from Harper's physician indicating she had but two weeks to live.

Accompanying the couple from their home in California was McGrew, a gardener and part-time student. When they arrived in Detroit, Kevorkian was still three months away from being charged with murder for offering his Mercitron to assist Janet Adkins' departure. A tempest was brewing in the teapot for Kevorkian would be criminally charged in Adkins' death.

The threesome checked into the Comfort Inn on August 18, 1990, in Romulus, Michigan on the western outskirts of the Motor City. By then, Harper had a malignant tumor on her liver and was intent on ending her cancer-ravaged life.

A DEADLY POTION

After checking into the motel, Harper changed her clothes and put on the things she wanted to wear when she died.

About 2:00 a.m., Harper took ten sleeping tablets as a sedative, Dalmane to be exact; alone, these pain killers were not enough to do the job. She then ingested some Dramamine, a motion-sickness pill, to fight nausea. Then to hasten the pills' metabolization, she washed everything down with Kahlua, a coffee liqueur.

Harper had been supplied this recipe for suicide from The Hemlock Society USA, a right-to-die organization. In 1988, the Harpers had joined the Society, advocating an individual's right to die in cases of extreme suffering or terminal illness. The Harpers belonged to The Hemlock Society USA because they believed in it.

Bob had brought a clear, plastic bag with him from California. "So many plastic bags are opaque," Bob said. "Ginger would want to be able to see us and for us to see her. She wanted a clear bag. So, I'd put one away years ago."

Harper lay down on the bed with her husband on one side of the bed and her daughter kneeling on the other. McGrew recalls, "We just talked and kissed and even laughed and had some loving moments and this went on for some time." Holding hands, the threesome said good night and good bye.

Then, Harper's shoulders were lifted up from the pillows so that the plastic bag could be slid beneath her head. Harper reached up to help bring the bag down over her head. But Harper soon became agitated, moving about. She was uncomfortably warm. "It's hot, it's hot," she complained. So the bag was removed.

"When the ten sleeping pills began to take effect," Bob recalls, "I tried to put the bag over her head twice more, but each time Ginger moved her hand and head."

McGrew explained, "I had asked mother on one or two occasions if she wanted to discontinue this, but she said, *No!*" By the third request, both McGrew and her stepfather were worn out.

"I am so afraid we will fail, yet I am ready to give up. I don't know what to do," McGrew worried to herself. "If we give up though, mother will either be made a vegetable by the drug overdose, or would wake up anguished because her plan didn't work and she would have to find another way. Then we will have to decide on some other plan. But we don't have any other plan and we don't know where to go if this fails."

They thought they were going to have to wait until morning. But, after another hour had passed, Harper's breathing became deeper and calmer. She had faded into unconsciousness. The medication had finally put her to sleep. Bob Harper decided, "I'll have to try the bag again because Ginger's biggest fear is that something would go wrong and that she wouldn't be able to exit the way she planned."

Bob Harper grumbled to himself, "This was supposed to be simple, painless and legal. For Ginger, that was supposed to be the whole point of it."

McGrew recalls, "At this point, my stepfather pulled the bag over mother's head and secured it."

By the time Bob Harper finally pulled the bag over his wife's head, he admittedly was pretty emotional and frazzled. He readily confessed that, in the end, it was he who took the initiative to replace the clear, plastic bag over his wife's head for the last time, but only after Harper finally became unconscious. To be sure, Bob also took it upon himself to secure that bag with a chain of six rubber bands which he had glued together. He then fastened the bag with metal twist-ties.

When she finally surrendered, her ordeal had dragged on for five hours. Her daughter was at her side. "I was lying on the bed next to my mother," McGrew recounted. "Her left hand was in my right hand. I was looking down at her feet."

Harper died around 7:00 a.m. and McGrew sobbed. "I left the room because at that point," McGrew said. "It was over and I . . . just broke down. I knew that my dad was having a hard enough time keeping it together and I didn't want to make it any worse for him. So I went to my room and cried."

After his wife died, Bob Harper summoned police. Before the police arrived, McGrew unfolded a note written by her mother to be read after she died:

Thank you Shanda darling, a million times over. I just love you.

Mom

THE POLICE CONFESSION

When the police arrived, Comfort Inn General Manager Julie Merritt took them to the Harper suite. Bob Harper was sitting in a red, stuffed chair by the window; Harper's body was found lying face-up on the left side of the bed, wearing blue knit slacks and a bra.

"Anything you say," Romulus Police Sergeant Daryl Poe warned McGrew and her stepfather, "can and will be used against you." But they gave little thought to this so-called *Miranda* warning.

The Romulus Police first asked McGrew to make a statement. As McGrew truly believed she had committed no crime, at least in Michigan, she freely talked. While she made her confession, her stepfather listened silently. For the next 22 minutes, she confessed to the Romulus Police while their tape machine whirled away, etching every word on magnetic tape.

The police officer demanded to know, "Who put the bag over Ginger's head, you or Shanda?"

"Let's put it this way. Just say it was me. I'm 72. Shanda's 40 in two more days. If there's any kickback on this thing, let it be mine, not Shanda's," Harper told police.

Then the police wanted to know, "Why did you put the bag over your wife's head?"

"If I didn't put the bag over her head," Bob explained, "she'd wake up and we'd be right back where we started from."

"Ginger wanted us to hold her hand when she went out," Bob stated. "That's why we chose Michigan. We spent close to $3,000 just to come here . . . just so we could hold her hand."

For the next 30 minutes, Harper rambled on, at one point telling police, "We thought it was going to be something so simple and quick and easy."

Bob was to regret making a statement to the police. Harper said in retrospect, "I never would have admitted helping my wife commit suicide if I had known police would consider Ginger's death a murder.

"I thought my statement was merely needed so police could make a complete report and we'd be free to leave. I never realized it could be considered a criminal confession. I thought it was just a routine police procedure -- like a traffic citation or whatever," Harper said. "Had I known that police were conducting a criminal investigation, I would have kept absolutely quiet until we had an attorney with us."

Harper had no regrets for helping his wife kill herself to avoid the agony of a protracted death from cancer. "I was doing what she wanted me to do," Harper offered. Unsympathetic, the prosecutor used these confessions against Harper.

AUTOPSY REPORT

Wayne County Deputy Coroner Sawait Kanluen observed a cancerous tumor on Harper's liver.

The autopsy report concluded that Harper did not die from the non-toxic amounts of the pain killer, sleeping pills and a nausea drug she had ingested. Rather, she died of asphyxiation from having a bag placed over her head.

Both confessions were taken to the prosecuting attorney who branded Harper's death a *mercy killing*. The prosecutor contended that Mrs. Harper would not have died . . . but for the bag having been placed over her head by her husband.

Assistant Prosecutor Timothy Kenny declared Harper had crossed the line from *assisting his wife* to *murdering her*. Kenny proclaimed, "When one person is responsible for taking the life of another, prosecutors have a duty to act." Despite Harper's suicide attempt, Kenny argued, "she died at the hands of the defendant."

Bob Harper was not allowed to leave Michigan, instead he was arrested and charged with murder and with conspiracy to commit murder. "The conspiracy charge refers to Harper's assistance of his wife's suicide," said Nancy Schutte, 34th District Court Administrator in Romulus.

Harper was jailed because he could not post the $25,000 cash bond. In the 34th District Court, Judge William Szlinis denied a request to lower the bond, fearing Harper would flee back to California before his trial.

Judge Szlinis returned Harper to the Wayne County Jail to await his preliminary examination, two weeks away. The defendant appeared tired, but managed a smile. Before he left the courthouse, Harper was handcuffed. "Not too tight," the old man asked the deputy sheriff.

Harper's defense attorney Hugh Davis suggested, "I don't think any jury is going to convict this man of anything. An act of love cannot be a crime. Whenever the law sets itself up against life -- the law fails."

Prosecuting Attorney John D. O'Hair admitted he did not think Harper should spend any time in jail. A plea bargain offer was made to Harper by the Wayne County Prosecutor's Office. If Harper had pled guilty, he would serve no jail time and, instead, would be placed on probation, doing community service in his home state of California.

Harper was steadfast that he had committed no crime. He refused to plea bargain, relying instead on his criminal defense attorneys, Otis Culpepper and Hugh Davis. His defense team acknowledged that going to trial was a risky business. "But the defense is simple -- *an act of love cannot be a crime*," explained attorney Davis. "We will try this case on the frontier between law and justice."

To help fund Harper's defense, The Hemlock Society USA raised $14,300. The Society promotes the right of the terminally ill to end their lives.[42] Derek Humphry, founder and national director of The Hemlock Society USA, declared, "This sends a message that legislators must modify the law regarding assisted suicides because the public wants this done." Humphry would later testify as a defense witness for Harper.

GUARDIAN ANGEL

After a week in the Wayne County Jail, a guardian angel from A-1 Bail Bond Services, Ltd. flew in from California and descended upon the Wayne County Jail bringing a $25,000 cash bond for Bob Harper. The Guardian Angel was someone Harper had never met.

At 1:45 p.m. on Sunday, Harper left jail a bit disoriented and still adjusting to his surroundings. McGrew, who had been held in the Romulus Police Department lockup for three days, was also released. Never formally charged, McGrew was named in Harper's felony warrant as an "unindicted co-conspirator to murder."

Harper's benefactor was Carl Wardlaw, 58, of Sacramento, California who stepped forward with his own $25,000 for Harper's bond. Free of charge. "Mr. Harper is not a criminal," Wardlaw protested, "he was just trying to do the right thing for someone he loved."

A bail bondsman for ten years, Wardlaw had never before put up bail on his own behalf to free a prisoner. "I bail out so many people who don't deserve it, people who probably belong where they are," Wardlaw complained. "But I don't think this man has broken a law in his life."

Wardlaw heard of Harper's plight from TV and news reports. "I used to be married and I loved my wife," Wardlaw reflected. "If she had ever been in that kind of situation, I would have wanted to do the same for her."

Wardlaw was not alone in volunteering Harper's bond: Joe Yeargain, 76, a retired Sacramento business executive, also offered to post Harper's bail.

FROM CRADLE TO GRAVE

McGrew spent a tearful 50 minutes on the witness stand, describing her mother's last moments in this world.

Lying next to her mother in bed, Shanda was cradling her mother, holding her hand, swallowing her own breath while waiting for the clear plastic bag over her mother's face to suffocate her. The prosecutor asked McGrew:

Prosecutor: Would *you* have pulled down the plastic bag over your mother's face if your stepfather had not done so?

McGrew: Yes. If necessary, *I* would have done it.

Charged with first degree murder, in his week-long trial Bob Harper took the witness stand on a Wednesday for 90 minutes to testify. Defense attorney Davis asked his client:

Davis: Do you love your wife?

Harper: Of course!
Davis: Would you do anything to hurt her?

| Harper: | No. |

Harper told the court how he felt compelled to assist his wife to complete her final exit. "It was the only thing I could do to carry out her trust in me," Harper confided. "It would be the most devastating thing in the world to Ginger if she had awakened."

"I had no choice," Harper testified, his voice cracking. "I realized that if I didn't do something to aid her, she was going to end up exactly the same way she did a year before."

THE JURY VERDICT

If found *guilty*, Harper's penalty in Michigan could be a sentence of up to life in prison. The week-long trial began on Monday. By Thursday of Harper's one-week trial, the defense had rested its case. In closing arguments to the jury, Defense Attorney Otis Culpepper petitioned jurors to explore a new frontier in assisted suicide. "When you consider the law, you don't give up your common sense," Culpepper observed, "you don't give up your human compassion."

Assistant Prosecutor Timothy Kenny retorted, "The poetry of his attorney's words does not elevate Harper's case to the level of an acquittal."

Judge Isidore Torres instructed the jury in the law. Defense Attorney Davis speculated about the jury, "I think they can only conclude that Harper's hand was carrying out Ginger's will."

One dozen jurors began deliberations. The initial vote, though a secret at the time, had been 8-4 for acquittal. McGrew began to fear for her stepfather. Twice the jury wrote a note to the judge asking him to redefine the term *second-degree murder*. "I was absolutely certain they were going to come back with a *guilty* verdict," McGrew confided. "It was just a surprise to me."

The jury failed to reach a verdict after an hour of deliberating on Thursday. The next day, Friday, May 10, the jury met for one more hour, and the 12 jurors reached a unanimous verdict. What the jury did reflected the mood of the country. They ignored the written statutes relying instead on their own *moral* law.

The jury foreperson read the verdict aloud, announcing that the 12 members found Harper *not guilty*. The jurors did not believe that Harper killed his wife. He only assisted her in taking the final steps in her own irreversible journey to suicide.

When the jury foreperson announced the *not guilty* verdict, Defense Attorney Davis declared triumphantly, "Happy Mother's Day."

Harper, with tears welling in his eyes, sighed deeply, "Thank God for that. It's over."

At hearing the *not guilty* verdict, McGrew gasped and then sobbed, as she threw her hands over her face. "We were certain it was going to be *guilty*," Shanda confessed and told reporters, "I just feel like Bob has been vindicated and my mother can rest in peace now. We love her. We feel she made the right decision. We're glad we went with her."

Bob Harper did not waver as he walked out of court a free man. "I'm glad the jurors could understand and feel the strain I was under that night," sighed Harper. "I knew in my heart that what I did for Ginger was right . . . but whether the law would see it that way or not, I didn't know."

Harper mused, "It's been eight months of strain and worrying, wondering what was going to happen. I wish I hadn't had the trial, but I don't regret what I did."

Harper said he would be devoting some of his time

to secure legislative passage of a bill supporting physician-assisted suicide. With his customary dry humor
somewhat restored, Harper mused that having a law
permitting doctors to assist in suicide is ". . .like having
a fire insurance policy: You hope you never have to
cash it in, but you sleep better knowing it's there." But
despite Harper's personal commitment, the California
ballot proposal #161 -- the "right-to-die" initiative for
which Bob Harper labored -- was defeated in November
1992.

One letter writer would have supported Harper's efforts.[43]

Dear Editor:

*I support the right-to-die bill. There should be
a bill on it, and it should be nobody's business but the person who is dying and their
family.*

Juror Dean Glossop, 26, a student at The University
of Michigan, voted to acquit Harper from the first, saying "Second degree murder is a very important law that
we don't want people breaking. But in this case, the
motivation was not to murder. In fact, to call this a
murder would be a miscarriage of justice. I feel a great
deal of sympathy for Mr. Harper. My decision was
based on the way the act was carried out."

Another juror, Leonard Hicks, 52, explained his concern: "I really don't feel that the charges should have
been brought. I had some compassion. We can never
say, if we got into this situation, 'Would we do this?' or
'Could we do this?' It's something you cannot say."

Looking at the broader questions, juror Jorge Garza,
31, said that the suffering of terminally ill people is a
situation that needs to be addressed nationally. "A lot

more people are going to face this situation," Garza warned.

Prosecutor O'Hair said that Harper's *not guilty* verdict would not make Michigan a haven for people who want to die. "Harper has gone through an ordeal and that, in and of itself, should be of some deterrent value."

Bertram Harper had persuaded a jury to permit those who assist suicides not only by giving patients the means to kill themselves but, also, by doing the actual killing. After his acquittal, Harper protested that he should not have had to endure such a court battle. "Physician-assisted suicide is something that should be done openly and above board by the medical society," Harper said.

But would Bertram Harper do the same thing again, knowing he would have to endure a nearly year-long ordeal? Harper professed, "If it meant ending my wife's suffering -- Yes!

"I knew in my heart what I did was right."

chapter four

Night on
Bald Mountain

Besides being born and paying taxes, each one of our lives crosses one common path . . . the road to dying. Sherry Miller and Marjorie Wantz met each other along that inevitable road. Though Kevorkian ushered them along, neither woman was terminally ill by most medical definitions. Without Kevorkian's assistance, neither would have died a natural death within six months.

Fearful he would be arrested and either Wantz or Miller would be left straggling by the side of that road, unattended, Kevorkian arranged for their double exit. As always, Dr. Death offered his services without charge.

MARJORIE WANTZ

Marjorie Wantz, 58, hailed from Sodus, Michigan near Benton Harbor. Her unbearable chronic pain resulted from a disorder due to pelvic abrasions. Housebound, she felt that no one understood the severity of her un-

remitting pain. The pain was intractable and she enjoyed no relief despite repeated visits to Mayo Clinic,
Cleveland Clinic and The University of Michigan Hospital in Ann Arbor.

Wantz had purchased the book, *Final Exit*.[44] Author
Derek Humphry, founder of The Hemlock Society USA
offers prescriptions for death -- including stock piling
drugs to die by overdose. Frustrated at her inability to
obtain such lethal drugs, Wantz complained, "A doctor
will *not* write a prescription for you. I know because
I've tried."

Fearful of a failed attempt at suicide, Wantz had said,
"If you do it yourself, you don't know what you're do-
ing." For the help Wantz needed, she would seek out
Kevorkian's assistance.

August 1991 had been a particularly bad month for
Wantz.   On August 5, she was hospitalized at Sinai
Hospital for vaginal pain. While there, Wantz stated her
"intent to kill herself if her pain cannot be eliminated or
managed," reported Dr. Linda Hotchkiss. "She has
sought many physical evaluations, but she has not completed a course of available non-narcotic medication at
therapeutic levels," Hotchkiss indicated. Indeed, Wantz
"refuses hospitalization for treatment of her depression,
which exacerbates her pain."

On August 16, Wantz and Kevorkian appeared together on the TV-2 *Dayna Eubanks* talk show in Detroit,
advocating physician-assisted suicide. Wantz was concerned that she would fail if she attempted suicide.
Initially, Kevorkian refused to assist her, insisting that
she pursue other available treatments which she did.

Nevertheless, twice during that month of August, ap-
plications were filed to commit Wantz involuntarily for
psychiatric evaluation. Some doctors had said Wantz
suffered from delusions, preventing her from believing

that pain control medication could aid her. Other doctors disagreed.

One physician said she was suffering from "major depression," while another doctor characterized Wantz as "an alert, cooperative person who presented herself logically and was able to stay on topic and has shown ability to think through options." In the end, the court refused to commit Wantz to a psychiatric institution and, instead, permitted her to return home.

Then, there was Miller.

SHERRY MILLER

After 12 years of multiple sclerosis, Miller had lost the use of her arms, leg and neck muscles. She was afraid of the pain in botching an attempt at suicide. Even if she had wanted to, Miller was incapable of ingesting a fatal dose of pills by herself. "I didn't want to do anything half ass," she proclaimed.

Miller, 41, of Roseville, Michigan had read about Kevorkian in a *Detroit Free Press Magazine* article and had seen Kevorkian on a TV talk show in the fall of 1989. "I don't know what I'll do if he isn't allowed to help me," she worried.

Miller, mother of two teenagers, began having suicidal ideations in 1983 after her divorce and after being crippled by multiple sclerosis. Her best friend, Sharon Welsh from Clinton Township, Michigan, had commented, "She was sad. Her whole life had changed."

Suicide was always lurking around in the back of her mind. This dilemma had haunted her private thoughts for nearly a decade -- to live in pain or make a rational choice to die! Miller was trapped in her body, kept alive only by the extraordinary means of others. Even on a good day she was very miserable. To end her life would be to spare those she loved as well.

In March 1990, Miller wrote to Kevorkian knowing that it would be done properly. *"His* is a sure way, a peaceful way," Miller reflected.

Despite her multiple sclerosis, in her first writing to Kevorkian, Miller wrote, in big letters . . . HELP! She asked the doctor to consider aiding her suicide and the two met several times. "He wanted to make sure of my medical condition. And he told me to get counseling and make sure that this is what I want to do. He was very cautious and kind."

Miller did see a therapist, but was still determined to die. While her friends were supportive, her family opposed her wish to end her life. Kevorkian never offered Miller the use of his Mercitron. Because Miller was afraid Kevorkian would say, "No." she never asked Dr. Death to employ his suicide machine.

MILLER TESTIFIES FOR KEVORKIAN

In January 1991, Miller testified in Kevorkian's defense at a trial before judge Gilbert. The court was considering whether the licensed M.D. should be ordered to stop using the Mercitron and stop assisting in suicides altogether.

Public sentiment was building in favor of Kevorkian as the opinion pages burgeoned with letters to the editor. One citizen wrote:[45]

Dear Editor:

Re: "Killer Kevorkian" from Roseville

I agree with this person: They should not call Jack Kevorkian "Doctor." The reason is because it does the man a great disservice.

Doctors, to me, are people who exploit people's illnesses. They treat you according to your medical insurance, not according to your disease, disability, or injury. And they don't give a whit whether you suffer or not -- as long as they get to keep you alive. Because only when you are alive are you "stock in trade" for them.

I suggest a new title for Kevorkian: Humanitarian.

At one point, Kevorkian had branded medicine an "ethically dead profession," discrediting its so-called leaders as "arrogant, greedy, deceitful, hypocritical wimps."

In Kevorkian's life, his father had died of sudden heart failure when Jack Kevorkian was 33, causing him to slip into a major depression. Nine years later, his mother died.

"Our mother suffered from cancer," says Kevorkian's sister, Janus. "I saw the ravages right up to the end. Her mind was sound, but her body was gone. My brother's option would have been more moral than all the Demerol that they poured into her, to the point that her body was all black and blue from the needle marks. She was in a coma and she weighed only 70 lbs. Even then I said to the doctor, *'This isn't right, to keep her on an IV,'* but he shrugged his shoulder and said, *'I'm bound by my oath to do that.'*"

Kevorkian's reflection on death is that "If you don't have any sort of faith, you think of the big nothingness. And you wonder: *What is this brief span of consciousness? What is all this?* There's no answer, anyway." When interrogated in court about what happens after death, Kevorkian professed, "You rot!"

But Miller had also testified about her own multiple sclerosis: "I should have done something sooner. I should have ended my life myself instead of waiting until I can't do anything on my own. I can't take a bottle of pills. I can't get to them. I need help with everything. I feel like a 42 year old baby."

Kevorkian struggled with Miller's inability to swallow pills reflecting that:

> *The first step was to decide on the method I was to use. Supplying drugs for the patient to swallow would be too much like active euthanasia. Then I recalled that in our medical school lectures on pathology the professor somewhat cynically remarked that carbon monoxide offers the best way to commit suicide. The pure gas has no color, taste, or smell; and it's toxic enough to cause rapid unconsciousness in relatively low concentration. Furthermore, in light complexioned people, it often produces a rosy color that makes the victim look better as a corpse.[46]*

But one of Kevorkian's arch-antagonists, Oakland County Medical Examiner Dr. Ljubisa Dragovic, had autopsied many of Kevorkian's medicide patients after-the-fact and disagreed. While *euthanasia* means easy death, Dragovic contended:

> *I can assure you . . .these were not all easy deaths. Poisoning by carbon monoxide in this fashion is not easy or quick. . . . It apparently took about ten minutes or more. It was probably less humane than the cyanide poisoning used in Auschwitz.*

Regardless of methodology, in February 1991, Judge Gilbert loathfully characterized Kevorkian as an arrogant, publicity hound seeking public recognition through bizarre behavior. Judge Gilbert then ordered Kevorkian to stop using the Mercitron and prohibited him from assisting in suicides.

But the judge's order was worth the paper it was written on because Prosecutor Thompson had no plans to prosecute Kevorkian even when the doctor later violated Judge Gilbert's injunctive prohibition.

THE NIGHT BEFORE

On Tuesday, October 22, 1991, the night before their deaths, Kevorkian set up his amateur video camera in the living room of Miller's Roseville, Michigan home. Ten participants huddled before the camera's lens, discussing the planned deaths of these two women.

The obitiatrist's "death counseling" protocol for prospective suicides was underway. Miller and Wantz were present with family, a few friends and Kevorkian. The atmosphere was very emotional.

Kevorkian casually twirled his glasses in hand, insisting of Miller, "So, what do you want? Put it in plain English."

"I have no qualms," asserted Wantz who suffered from multiple sclerosis. "I want to die. I've tried to kill myself three different times. . . tried everything short of a gun. This time," gazing warmly at Kevorkian, though in chronic pain from a pelvic inflammation, "it's got to be done right."

A tree-lined, dirt road led to the small, rustic cabin sitting on the lake shore at the Bald Mountain State Recreation Area, near Pontiac, Michigan north of Detroit. A double exit was planned for this night on Bald Mountain.

Kevorkian had rented the cabin. Total cost was $70 for two nights. No electricity. Fresh well water from a pump. The outhouse was conveniently nearby. A fire in the wood stove could take the October chill from the night air. A hungry person might have cooked their last supper on the open-air grill. While bunk beds were available as a modest accommodation for groups of 20 or so, Wantz and Miller were to die while resting on cots. In the cabin on Bald Mountain that night were Kevorkian and his sister, Janus, William Wantz (the husband of Marjorie Wantz), Miller and her friends Welsh and Karen Nelson.

On Wednesday, October 23, 1991, Wantz made her final exit, but not before writing Kevorkian a suicide note . . . part of which read:

Jack Kevorkian:

I, Marjorie Wantz, want everyone to know that this is my decision and no one else's. After 3-1/2 years I cannot go on with this pain and agony. I have not been out of the house in 3-1/2 years except to go to Detroit to the doctor.

I do not call this living, never getting out. What is it like to go to the grocery store or go for a walk?

I'm so glad there's Dr. Kevorkian who can help me. I have begged him to help me for two years. But the last year, I should say 13 months, have been pure hell. No doctor can help me any more. If God won't come to me, I'm going to find God. I can't stand it any longer.

Wantz was then connected to the Mercitron and received an injection of lethal drugs. She died at 5:05 p.m. with her husband nearby.

Miller was fitted with a Kevorkian-designed face mask and connected by a tube to a cylinder bottle of carbon monoxide which was resting on the cabin floor.

Just before Miller died, Welsh whispered to her, "I love you." And Miller replied, "I love you too." At 6:15 p.m., Miller simply breathed in a lethal dose of carbon monoxide and went to sleep . . . forever.

About 7:07 p.m., Wednesday, October 23, Kevorkian telephoned the Oakland County Sheriff's Department to report a "double doctor-assisted suicide." The doctor indicated to deputies that the suicides were "physician-assisted" and that he was the only doctor in attendance.

Though still forced to act alone, Kevorkian knew that there were medical practitioners who would join his cause . . . if they did not fear criminal prosecution or loss of their physician's license.

Sally Hess, park secretary, observed the scene on the morning after the night at Bald Mountain. "There wasn't anything gory or bloody, so there was nothing to clean up."

CIRCLE OF SILENCE

After the double exit, relatives and others who were present when the two women died were taken into custody and whisked away by deputy sheriffs; though separated from each other, the survivors all closed together in a circle of silence. They refused to give statements to the sheriff about their version of events. "The only witnesses are people who won't talk and two ladies who are dead," grumbled Assistant Prosecutor Michael Modelski. The authorities were stumped.

The witnesses' hesitancy impeded Prosecutor Thompson's investigation. The prosecutor was having difficulty establishing what actually happened. "One of the biggest problems is that the people who were present are not telling us anything . . . so the investigation is going to take a while," admitted Modelski.

"That's right, they won't talk to him because he's a lunatic," Kevorkian's attorney Fieger said of Modelski. "He's the guy who tried Kevorkian for murder. Who's going to help him?"

To break the circle of silence, Thompson went on a "fishing expedition," casting his net of subpoenas out to cover everyone who might have been told anything by anyone. The penalty was stiff for witnesses who would refuse to testify before his grand jury.

If a grand jury witness invoked the Fifth Amendment -- seeking protection from self-incrimination by refusing to testify -- the prosecutor could forcibly afford such reluctant witness immunity from prosecution. Once immunity was granted, witnesses who still persisted in remaining silent could be jailed until they testified; the keys to the jailhouse then would be held by the obstinate witness. Once having been granted immunity, the silent witness was at no risk of self-incrimination.

Prosecutor Thompson subpoenaed several people suspected of being in the cabin during that night on Bald Mountain: Kevorkian, Janus, Welsh, Nelson and William Wantz.

"It's a question of the proximate cause of death," Thompson instructed. "That is the question a grand jury will have to decide before voting on whether to indict Kevorkian."

A POLITICAL ISSUE

With a stoic Dr. Death at his side, Kevorkian's lawyer launched a vigorous attack against the prosecutor, berating him as an "arch-Machiavellian manipulator", "an evil ghoul", a "fascist" and "a malignant despot"; or at other times, Fieger painted the prosecutor as a "certified raving loon" and "insane."

At a news conference, Fieger proffered a poster of Prosecutor Thompson with a red balloon for a nose, denouncing the prosecutor as a "first class buffoon." Fieger couldn't care less that he offended Thompson and others by pasting a clown nose on the prosecutor's picture asking, "Do people — every time they look at Dick Thompson — think of him with that nose on his face? Absolutely! Is it trite? Yes. Is it beneath me? Perhaps. It is unprofessional? Perhaps. But was it effective? Absomotherf---lutely!"

In reply, Thompson tagged Fieger's remarks as "absurd, ridiculous and slanderous."

Thompson later came under fire from his opponent in the 1992 political race for the job of Oakland County Prosecutor. Candidate Steven Kaplan challenged Thompson for the prosecutor position. Kaplan attacked Thompson by running on a platform that criticized Thompson's repeated prosecutions of Kevorkian.

Kaplan argued in favor of physician-assisted suicide, though under "controlled circumstances," where a patient suffers from terminal illness or chronic pain. "It's a liberty issue," Kaplan posited.

In the next November election, the prosecutor's political opponent, riding principally on a pro-Kevorkian platform, failed to unseat Richard Thompson; however, Thompson's reelection margin of victory was much narrower than other Republicans running for county-wide office in the same election..

One constituent, Keith B. Braun of West Bloomfield, Michigan wrote a message to Oakland County Prosecutor Richard Thompson, saying that Thompson's narrow margin of victory sent a "strong message from Oakland County voters that we want him to devote his resources and our tax dollars to law enforcement and not personal vendettas."[47]

NOT LICENSED TO KILL

Less than one month after Miller and Wantz expired, the Michigan Board of Medicine suspended Kevorkian's license as a physician at the request of Michigan Attorney General Frank Kelly. In an opinion (August 21, 1992), the board justified their action, charging that Kevorkian's use of drugs with both Janet Adkins and Wantz violated Michigan's public health code.

Kevorkian was then still licensed in California where he had been allowed to practice medicine since 1957. But in 1993, California authorities revoked his medical license insisting that doctors "do not assist people in committing suicide." California Administrative Law Judge, M. Gayle Askren, conceded, "I don't think what I do is really going to stop what he's doing."

Fieger rebuked the judge and board as "a religious cult on the order of Branch Davidian West. The only difference between David Koresh and that [administrative law] judge is that the judge probably shaves. We would prefer that the judge and the medical board burn themselves to death like the Branch Davidians. They'll go to hell anyway, so they might as well do it sooner." One letter to the *Detroit Free Press* editor lamented:[48]

Dear Editor:
For all his good intentions, Dr. Jack Kevorkian is fighting an uphill battle, because the medical community has a vested interest in keeping you alive.

Whatever the cost to you and your family, whatever pain and agony you suffer, however

*humane and sensible the alternatives, they'll
find a way to ruin your death.*

E.P. Michalke

THE ARREST

Three months after Wantz and Miller made their final
exit, on February 3, 1992, a 17-person, Oakland County
Citizens Grand Jury indicted Kevorkian in their deaths.

Both of the women had sought aid in dying. While
Kevorkian responded, he was not treated as any Good
Samaritan but, rather, was prosecuted as their killer.
"What I'm doing may be theologically immoral,"
Kevorkian explained, "but medically, it is absolutely ethi-
cal. Nothing matters to me except the suffering human
in front of me. . . .We didn't study sacredness in medi-
cal school."

After the grand jury indictment was handed down,
sheriff deputies patrolled downtown Royal Oak on the
lookout for Kevorkian. About 9:30 a.m., the sheriff
spotted Kevorkian driving toward his Main Street apartment. The deputies pulled him over in his VW camper
bus and escorted him to the patrol car like any common
criminal. Under arrest and in handcuffs, the officers
took Kevorkian before the nearest circuit judge.

"So much has been heaped on me," Kevorkian said.
"But, even if everybody's against me, if there's just one
patient who needs my help -- even if they throw me in
jail -- I would help that one patient." And if the authorities jailed Kevorkian, he vowed a hunger-strike to
starve himself to death.

Sheriff deputies dragged Kevorkian before Oakland
County Circuit Judge Richard Kuhn, charging him with
two counts of open murder and one count of illegally
delivering drugs. Judge Kuhn set a $10,000 (or 10 per-

cent) bond, releasing Kevorkian on the condition he not assist anyone else in suicide.

Asked if he felt any guilt, the doctor asserted, "No. I feel no more guilt than any physician who performs a medical service. Guilt is wrongdoing. I have no guilt."

Karen Nelson, a friend of Miller who was in the cabin that night on Bald Mountain, fumed over Kevorkian's arrest protesting, "I think it's ridiculous, just utterly stupid."

MUDDY WATERS

In February 1992, the *Detroit Free Press* conducted a poll of Michigan residents. Kevorkian is no murderer, respondents declared. By a 10-1 margin, Oakland County, Michigan residents would acquit Kevorkian if only they were to sit in judgment on his jury. Indeed, 60 percent of Detroit area residents favored a law allowing physicians to help in suicides.

"That's terrific," Kevorkian proclaimed when told of poll results. "But it's not going to have any effect on those dodos in Lansing" in the state legislature.

"Those polls aren't worth the power to blow them up with," countered State Senator Fred Dillingham, R-Fowlerville, sponsor of a bill criminalizing assisted suicide.

State Senator Lana Pollack, D-Ann Arbor, also protested saying any bill outlawing assisted suicide ". . .flies in the face of public opinion, common sense and current practice."

But it was neither the pollsters nor state senators nor potential jurors who would decide Kevorkian's fate this time. After the 17-person grand jury indicted Kevorkian, it was Rochester, Michigan District Judge James Sheehy who ultimately would rule.

In the courtroom, there was standing-room only. *Court TV* would nationally televise the unusual weekend hearing. "I'm not intimidated by this," Kevorkian defiantly declared. Kevorkian's congregation of supporters packed the church-like pews.

Assistant Prosecutor Lawrence J. Bunting summarized the state's position by saying, "We don't know where Kevorkian is going next. . . . What's going to stop him? . . . . He's uncontrollable." Bunting told the court, "The law is clear."

But, if the law is so clear, then why was Kevorkian being charged in the dual deaths of Wantz and Miller when, *nearly two years earlier,* the murder charge against Kevorkian in Adkins' death had been dismissed? If the law is so clear, then wasn't it the prosecutor who was muddying the waters?

"PARANOID FANTASY"

The behind-the-scenes judicial drama took a bizarre twist. Initially unaware, Judge Sheehy uncovered an unauthorized, clandestine investigation of himself undertaken by the prosecutor's office.

Two assistant prosecutors and a sergeant from the sheriff's office had interrogated one of Sheehy's clerks. These authorities were probing rumors that Sheehy had formed a preconceived notion in favor of defendant Kevorkian. Little did they know.

After questioning, the clerk disregarded the investigators' admonition not to discuss the interrogation. The clerk went public.

Judge Sheehy protested that, "The integrity of the court has been breached." But the prosecutor's office blasted the judge for concocting a "paranoid fantasy" while the prosecutor's office publicly denied any wrongdoing.

chapter five

Two Sides of a Coin

T hough not formally trained in the law, Kevorkian was a scholar in whatever single-minded tasks he undertook. He had researched the law before agreeing to help his first patient Janet Adkins. The oldest case law that Kevorkian could find reported in Michigan lawbooks was the decades-old, 1920 murder case of *People v Roberts*[49] decided by the Michigan Supreme Court.

When she died, just before the Great Depression, Katie Roberts was only 30. Like several of the women Kevorkian would help with their own suicides, Katie Roberts had been diagnosed with multiple sclerosis.

One year later, on July 20, 1920, the several justices of the Michigan Supreme Court solemnly convened in the state capitol of Lansing to hear the appeal of her husband, convicted murderer Frank C. Roberts.

Sitting at the counsel table in the hallowed Supreme Court chambers was Roberts' attorney, James H. Pound of Detroit. Across from the aisle were the opposing counsel, Assistant Attorney General Alexander J. Groesbeck and Prosecuting Attorney Virgil W. McClintic from Mt. Pleasant.

Little more than one year earlier, Roberts, 36, a garage-attendant, had pled guilty to assisting in his ailing wife's suicide; the prosecutor had charged Roberts with murdering his wife. The trial judge, who had accepted defendant Roberts' guilty plea, had determined the degree of murder without impaneling a jury. There had been little mystery about defendant Roberts' guilt: he had readily confessed to prosecutor McClintic.

McClintic charged Roberts with murder by means of poison. "A husband who mixes Paris Green with water and places it within reach of his wife to enable her to end her suffering by ending her life is guilty of *murder by means of poison*," McClintic would argue, "even though this wife requested her husband to do so."

By now, far and away from Katie Roberts' final resting place, the hushed courtroom of the Michigan Supreme Court was slowly filling with spectators. A parade of justices filed in for that day's session.

Among the first to enter was Justice Bird, who later delivered the court's opinion. "Defendant Roberts was adjudged guilty of murder in the first degree in the Isabella County Circuit Court on his plea of confession and on the testimony which was taken by the court. Defendant Roberts alleges several errors occurred. We think not," Justice Bird was heard to say.

Roberts' mind wandered back to the death of his beloved wife one year earlier. Less than two weeks after young Katie Roberts had poisoned herself, her husband was arrested on an open charge of murder. Prosecutor McClintic filed his criminal complaint against Roberts on June 14, 1919.

AN ARREST IS MADE

Nine days later, on June 25, after a warrant had been issued, defendant Roberts was apprehended and brought before a justice of the peace. "You have the right for this court to conduct a preliminary examination," the justice of the peace instructed Roberts.

A preliminary exam would have required Prosecutor McClintic to present evidence to prove that the crime of murder was committed and that there was probable cause to believe that defendant Roberts had committed that crime. Instead, Roberts waived a preliminary examination. Roberts was bound over to the Isabella County Circuit Court on an open charge of murdering his desperately ill and long-suffering wife.

On July 12, Roberts appeared before Circuit Judge Ray Hart and was formally arraigned on an open charge of murder. Judge Hart read the Information to Roberts: "You are charged with the crime of *Murder by Means of Poison*. The People of the State of Michigan allege that -- at the request of your wife -- you mixed Paris Green, a substance containing arsenic, with water and placed it within her reach to enable her to commit suicide. Do you understand this charge and do you appreciate that you are accused of murder?"

Roberts was clear about what the gravity of the situation was. "Yes, I understand the charge is murder. However, I would like the court to appoint an attorney to represent me," Roberts requested.

Judge Hart acknowledged Roberts' request. The court then summoned and appointed attorney Dusenberry, an experienced lawyer. Dusenberry arrived at the courthouse and was allowed some considerable time that day to be spent counseling Roberts about the law. But only hours later that very same day, defendant Roberts and his counsel returned to the courtroom, ready for Roberts to plead *guilty*.

Defense Lawyer Dusenberry had advised the circuit judge that Roberts intended to plead guilty. The judge addressed defendant Roberts, "You have had an attorney appointed. Are you present with that attorney and are you ready to plead now to the charge?"

"Yes, sir," Roberts reported to the judge.

"What is your plea?" the court asked.

"Guilty as charged," Roberts confessed.

Defense Attorney Dusenberry was quick to interject, "Your Honor, Mr. Roberts' father is here and I wish you would talk to him and then you can talk to the defendant in private."

The judge conferred, off the record, with Roberts' father, then spent some time with defendant Roberts himself. By then, the prosecutor's chief witness, arrived in court. The judge reconvened the proceeding and Dr. Michael F. Bronstetter, Isabella County Coroner, was called to the witness stand to testify.

BODY EXHUMED FOR AUTOPSY

After exhuming Katie's body, the county coroner went to Stinson's Funeral Home to perform an autopsy. In attendance were Katie's three brothers, a six-person coroner's petit jury and the local news reporters. The coroner testified at Roberts' hours-long trial.

"I am the coroner of Isabella County," Bronstetter stated. "I presided at the inquest upon the body of Katie Roberts, whom I knew in her life. I knew her as the wife of Roberts. I was the surgeon who opened up the body and I examined her stomach and other intestinal organs."

"In what condition was the stomach, as you found it?" prosecutor McClintic inquired.

"The stomach was greatly dilated with gas and partly with fluid, in the amount of eight ounces; otherwise it was in a good state of preservation," Bronstetter reported.

"Did there seem to be any other substance in her stomach when you took it out of the body?" the prosecutor probed.

"There was a greenish substance in the stomach and some in the esophagus," Bronstetter recalled.

"What did you do with the stomach?" the prosecutor persisted.

"I tied it at both ends, before removing it, so as not to spill the contents, placed it in a glass container and personally took it with the other organs to the Michigan Board of Health at Lansing," Bronstetter explained.

"What did the analysis of that stomach show?" Prosecutor McClintic queried.

"The stomach showed 84 hundredths of an ounce of Paris Green," coroner Bronstetter detailed. "From the condition of the body and the amount of Paris Green found in the stomach, I would say the cause of death was aceto-arsenical poison," the coroner calculated.

Dr. Bronstetter had identified the body as that of Katie Roberts, wife of Frank Roberts. Indeed, the doctor had treated Katie as a patient. "About three or four months before Katie's death," the coroner recalled, "I saw her at her home where she and her husband lived. Katie was practically bed-ridden at that time. She was unable to do any kind of work. I don't even know whether she could get up and around. Her body was considerably wasted. She showed evidence of a long, drawn-out sickness. She showed symptoms of multiple sclerosis."

Defense attorney Dusenberry asked Bronstetter to explain the disease known as M.S. "Multiple Sclerosis is a disease of the central nervous system, affecting both the brain and spinal cord. The cause of these patches in the brain and cord is unknown. Katie Roberts had the outward signs of multiple sclerosis: the rapid pulse, hesitating, singsong speech."

The coroner described that Katie Roberts was practically helpless, indeed, a hopeless patient terminally ill, without chance of recovery. "I considered her case as incurable," Dr. Bronstetter concluded, handing over to the court his written Coroner's Report. These coroner's findings were accepted as Exhibit A and admitted into evidence. Bronstetter stepped down from the witness stand.

ACCUSED TESTIFIES

Roberts then insisted on taking the stand to testify in his own defense. He was sworn to tell the truth, then carefully seated himself in the witness chair.

Frank and Katie met in northern Illinois before both clans moved to mid-Michigan.

The family finances had been stretched since Katie had become more seriously ill. The family unit had disintegrated. Katie was forced to live in Mount Pleasant with her father-in-law while Roberts and his son, Onie, slept at the garage where Roberts worked as a mechanic. Roberts didn't mention the other three children.

"I never had the blues in my life," Roberts said, warding off suspicion that he was a man driven to hasten his wife's death. "But since there has been so much sickness in my family, I have had a hard time making both ends meet."

The year before, Katie was deteriorating and Roberts had traveled south with Katie the 100 miles or more to Ann Arbor. Roberts described how Dr. Bronstetter had consented to send Katie Roberts to Ann Arbor, Michigan for treatment.

"I took her myself," Roberts recalled. "Katie was there 30 days, I think. I did not stay in Ann Arbor while she was there. I took her myself, made three trips down to see her while she was there and I brought

Katie back myself. I paid the expenses incident to her going to the hospital and staying there the 30 days. It wasn't paid by the county like Dr. Bronstetter said; I paid it out of my own pocket."

Defense Attorney Dusenberry interrogated his client further about Katie Roberts. "Had Katie ever tried to commit suicide before?"

"Yes, sir," Roberts replied.

"When was that?" Dusenberry demanded.

"Last summer. Yes, the summer of 1919," Roberts recollected. "She tried to kill herself with carbolic acid," a powerful disinfectant.

"So by her previous actions," Dusenberry pressed, "you knew that she was desirous of dying?"

"Yes, sir," Roberts solemnly stated.

Prosecutor McClintic studied the police report like a map. A local newspaper reported one of the Roberts' children as telling police that "papa gave mama something green."

POLICE CONFESSION

The authorities were quick to finger Roberts. "Her case was hopeless," Roberts had told police. "Katie asked me to get her something to put her out of her misery. Several times that morning, she had asked me to mix up some Paris Green that was there and give it to her."

The police report continued, "Finally I took the sack of Paris Green . . . and poured it into a tin cup. Then I filled the cup partly full of water and stirred it up and put it on a chair beside the cot that she was laying on. I walked out into the kitchen. I was out in the kitchen possibly ten minutes and then went back into her room. She had taken the Paris Green. Katie told me she had drunk it." It was shortly before noon.

By mid-afternoon, Roberts collected up the four children to keep vigil at their mother's bedside. Three hours later, she expired.

Prosecutor McClintic then cross-examined Roberts about the death of his wife. "On May 23, 1919, at your wife's request, you mixed a quantity of Paris Green in a cup and placed it on a chair near her side?"

"Yes, sir," defendant Roberts confessed to the prosecutor. "I told you that before. My wife had requested me to do that, so she could drink it. After that, she drank the Paris Green," Roberts freely admitted. "A few hours later, Katie died."

Hearing his admission, the judge had a private conference with Roberts. No jury was ever convened. Nonetheless, without a jury and that very same day, the court elected to sentence criminal defendant Roberts. The judge pronounced sentence:

The court has heard your plea of guilty to killing and murdering your wife, Mr. Roberts. The court has also heard testimony and seen the evidence introduced, bearing upon the degree of the crime charged.

The court hereby determines that you have committed murder in the first degree and judgment will be rendered accordingly. There is only one sentence that can be pronounced upon you, of course. The statute provides that, where murder shall be perpetrated by means of poison, that shall be murder in the first degree and the punishment shall be confinement in the state prison.

It is beyond my comprehension how a human being of normal conditions can commit such a crime as you have, Mr. Roberts, by placing poison within reach of your wife knowing her intention of committing suicide. You are a principal to the crime of murder.

Yours was, indeed, an inhuman and dastardly act. The sentence of this court is that you be confined to the state prison in Marquette, Michigan for the period of your natural life, at hard labor and in solitary confinement.

Defense Attorney Dusenberry was shocked. He had been led to believe that the court merely would accept Roberts' guilty plea. Dusenberry then thought that the court would set the matter for a jury trial, allowing a jury of Roberts' peers to decide whether Roberts was guilty of felony of first degree murder or some lesser included offense. Instead, the judge unilaterally had sentenced Roberts to life in prison, at hard labor, in solitary confinement.

Dusenberry had sought a jury trial as to the degree of murder committed by Roberts. Because that jury trial was denied, Defense Attorney Dusenberry appealed the case.

FINAL DECISION

Now, Justice Bird of the Michigan Supreme Court was about to render his opinion on this appeal. More than one year after Roberts had confessed to assisting Katie's suicide, the Michigan Supreme Court, seeming so removed from tiny, rural Isabella County, was to review the first degree murder conviction in appeal.

Justice Bird offered the Michigan Supreme Court's unanimous opinion: "If Roberts is convicted by confession, the trial court properly proceeded to examine witnesses to determine the degree of his crime. Roberts was not entitled to a jury of his peers because he had so readily confessed to the truth of the matter."

These justices were telling Roberts that he voluntarily sacrificed his constitutional right to have the jury determine the degree of his guilt . . . because Roberts had confessed. His plea of confession had made a criminal trial unnecessary. There was nothing else for the court to do but apply the statute and classify his crime.

Defendant's attorney argued, "There is no evidence that a crime was committed. Suicide is not a crime in Michigan. Katie Roberts committed no offense when she killed herself. If she, as principal, committed no offense, then neither did her husband, Roberts."

The high court was unpersuaded. Justice Bird explained, "If we were living in a purely common law atmosphere with a strictly common law practice and Roberts were charged as an accessory to suicide, your argument would be more persuasive. But Roberts is not charged as accessory to the offense of suicide.

"Frank Roberts is charged with *murder by means of poison*. He confessed that he mixed poison with water and placed it within his wife's reach, at her request. The important question is this: did Roberts' actions constitute *murder by means of poison?*" Justice Bird asked. Reaching for the Michigan statutes, Justice Bird slowly opened the book and quoted:

All murder perpetrated by poison shall be deemed murder of the first degree and punished by solitary confinement at hard labor in the state prison for life.

Justice Bird then closed the lawbook and reached for another treatise. Taking in hand an encyclopedia of common law, Justice Bird reflected on the laws of merry old England, which were not so merry:

Where one person advises, aids, or abets another to commit suicide and the other kills himself and the adviser is present when the suicide occurs, the adviser is guilty of murder as a principal; or if two persons mutually agree to kill themselves together and the means employed to produce death take effect upon one only, the survivor is guilty of murder of the one who dies.

A person may now be convicted of murder for advising a suicide, whether absent or present at the time it is committed, provided the suicide is the result of his advice.

Justice Bird then closed that old encyclopedia of law, reaching for a hornbook on the principles of common law. The hornbook was sandwiched by two covers, made of flattened animal horns which protected its contents. Justice Bird read from the hornbook:

He who kills another--at his own desire or command--is a murderer as much as if he had done it of his own hand.

Quietly, Justice Bird closed the hornbook and reflected. "It is immaterial whether Katie Roberts swallowed the poison willingly, intending thereby to commit suicide, or was overcome by force or overreached by fraud. True, the atrocity of the crime, in a moral sense, would be greatly diminished by the fact Katie Roberts' suicide was intended."

DR. DEATH

Justice Bird peered down from the bench through his horn-rimmed glasses saying, "The lives of all are equally under the protection of the law and under that protection to their last moment. The life of Katie Roberts, which had become a burden to her — hopelessly diseased -- is also under the protection of the law, equally as the lives of those who are in the full tide of life's enjoyment and anxious to continue to live.

"Purposely and maliciously to kill a human being, by administering to her poison, is declared by the law to be murder, irrespective of the wishes or the condition of Katie Roberts.

"If the prisoner furnished the poison to his wife for the purpose and with the intent that she should commit suicide and she accordingly took and used it for that purpose, then Roberts administered the poison to her within the meaning of the statute."

Having recited all of this law to the courtroom of spectators and attorneys, Justice Bird had steeled himself to deliver the final opinion of the Michigan Supreme Court with regard to prisoner Roberts.

"When Frank Roberts mixed the Paris Green with water and placed it within reach of his wife to enable her to put an end to her suffering by putting an end to her life, Roberts was guilty of *murder by means of poison*, even though Katie Roberts requested her husband to do so," Justice Bird calmly declared. "By this act, Frank Roberts deliberately placed within his wife's reach the means of taking her own life, which she could have obtained in no other way by reason of her helpless condition."

By Justice Bird, the Michigan Supreme Court declared that the 1919 judgment of conviction of Roberts was affirmed.

In 1923, after serving four years in Marquette State Prison, Roberts was released from prison. Michigan's

Governor Albert Sleeper had commuted Roberts' life sentence.

That remained the law in Michigan . . . until the year 1983 when Steven Campbell was tried for aiding a suicide.

chapter six

Just Shooting Blanks

After the *Roberts* decision was handed down, another Michigan court took a totally opposite view of assisted suicide. Indeed, Kevorkian had read the more recent case of *People v Campbell* before he ever assisted Janet Adkins in her medicide. Kevorkian ultimately ended his legal research by concluding, "My view -- that assisting a suicide is not murder -- was based on a recent case in Michigan" involving a defendant named *Campbell*.[50]

It was 1981 in the quiet courtroom of the circuit court for St. Clair County, Michigan. The courthouse in Port Huron stood proudly on the banks of the St. Clair River, the shipping artery to Lake Huron, in the heart of the St. Lawrence Seaway.

"Steven Paul Campbell, you have been bound over to this circuit court on an open murder charge in connection with a suicide death of Kevin Patrick Bashnaw," Judge James T. Corden advised. "How do you plead?"

"Your honor," Defense Attorney Sharon Parrish intervened, "Defendant moves to quash the information and dismiss this case on ground that providing a weapon to a person, who subsequently uses it to commit suicide, does not constitute crime of murder."

The prosecutor and the trial court had read the 1919 case of *People v Roberts* in justifying the trial of Campbell on an open charge of murder. Judge Corden considered defendant Campbell's motion and denied it. Campbell was to be tried for murdering Bashnaw -- who actually had committed suicide.

MERCURIAL TEMPER

Campbell's father was a drinker with a bad back. His mother worked the front desk at a motel. After Campbell cannon-balled down the hallowed halls of Port Huron High School, he got tagged as a ninth grade dropout with an attitude kept well-lubricated by alcohol and drugs. After four criminal arrests, his record was not quite as long as your arm.

Jill Campbell's name was tattooed on her husband's hand. In 1977, Campbell was 19 when he married 17-year-old Jill. Two babies quickly followed. Jill remembers, "I used to get beat all the time, even when I was pregnant."

Campbell and his buddy Kevin Bashnaw were best friends. Campbell's wife, and Bashnaw's girlfriend, Kimberly Cleland, were also best friends. They all spent time together.

Bashnaw was born at the tail end of a family of 12 children. He just wanted to get a job and survive. "He was happy-go-lucky and quiet," his twin-sister, Karen recalls.

Jill Campbell thought Bashnaw was gentle and considerate. Secretly, she had talked about divorcing her husband and running off to California with Bashnaw and her two children.

One time, Campbell and Bashnaw had swapped partners for sex. Jill took Bashnaw and Cleland grumbles, "I got stuck with Steve."

In September 1980, Campbell headed over to the house of his good friend, Bashnaw.

Campbell had been suspicious for some weeks that his wife and best buddy had become a little too close. Perhaps she was cheating on him. Campbell spied into Bashnaw's window, only to catch him in bed, making love to Jill. Stealing into the bedroom, Campbell watched for a while, until his car keys jangled, startling the couple.

"Hi," Bashnaw sheepishly said.

"Uh, oh," Jill exclaimed.

Campbell yanked his wife away from Bashnaw and "bitch-slapped" her. When Bashnaw intervened with apologies, Campbell suddenly chilled out, telling Bashnaw to forget all about it.

That night in this farming village west of Port Huron, they all partied down, guzzling a case and a half of beer. Campbell and Bashnaw hallucinated after smoking some peyote.

By the time Campbell and his wife went to bed, there was a dark cloud arising, just before dawn. "I'll get even with you and your lover-boy," the irate husband proclaimed. Before a week had passed, Jill knew that was no threat, but a promise.

BREAKFAST OF CHAMPIONS

A few weeks later, on Friday, October 3, Campbell had the "Breakfast of Champions" -- two beers, no Wheaties.

Still stinging from his earlier suspicions about Bashnaw and his wife, Campbell grabbed a 32 ounce beer and went hunting for his wife. In between gulps, he toked on a joint of marijuana.

Campbell was not far wrong. His wife and her friend, Cleland, met Bashnaw for lunch at a bar in Memphis, Michigan near the Vlasic pickle plant.

After lunch, Bashnaw returned to work and the girls drove out of town, finding Campbell staggering along the roadway. "He was pissed severely," Cleland remembers and wanted to know what Jill was up to.

Suddenly Campbell's schizoid mood shifted and he shrugged, "What the hell. Who's going to buy the beer?" Jill was, so she bought her husband a couple of six packs and they spent the rest of the afternoon arguing about Bashnaw.

About 11 p.m., Campbell left his wife at home with the kids and found his way over to Bashnaw's single-story home on Rabidue Road. Bashnaw and his roommate rented the place for $200 per month. A small party was going down.

By 1:30 a.m., nobody was left except Bashnaw, Campbell and his wife's friend, Cleland. The boys were ugly drunk and tripping on mescaline. Campbell was hollering about catching Bashnaw and Jill in the act. Time and again, Campbell commanded Bashnaw to just stay away from his wife. The arguing subsided.

"Steve and Kevin were about equally intoxicated at this point," Cleland later told police. Indeed, when Bashnaw's body was found the next day, the deceased's blood alcohol level was found to be 0.26 percent, two and one-half times higher than the level considered to be drunk driving.

Bashnaw had slipped into a dark mood, mumbling about his problems. His car was all broken down. And worse, Bashnaw's mom had fixed in her mind that Bashnaw had robbed a store recently. She was wrong, but Bashnaw couldn't convince her otherwise.

Just Shooting Blanks

They talked of heaven and hell. Campbell promised Bashnaw he would burn in hell. Bashnaw promised that if he went to hell, he would spend eternity getting drunk and playing poker.

Bashnaw began talking to Cleland and Campbell about committing suicide. "He was saying he was fed up, you know, fed up with the whole thing and he was going to shoot himself," Cleland testified. She tried unsuccessfully to change the subject away from suicide.

Bashnaw had never talked about suicide before. But at some point, Bashnaw came to the profound realization that "I don't have no gun."

Though Campbell had a sawed-off shotgun and a pistol at his parent's house, at first he said, "You can't *borrow* my gun. Man, I wouldn't even *sell* you one of my guns," Campbell touted.

"No, that's all right. I'll do it my way," Bashnaw concluded. His way would be to shoot himself while sitting in his favorite chair, blasting the stereo on hard rock station WLLZ-FM and high on peyote.

Making a "gun" with his left hand, pointing to his left temple, Bashnaw yelled, "Look at me. I must be crazy. You two are the only ones who ever heard me talk like this and here I've had it planned out for two weeks."

Though Bashnaw hesitated, Campbell persisted. "All right, Kevin," Campbell told him, "Tell you what, I'll sell you a gun. How much money you got on you now?"

Bashnaw counted all of his cash in the house. He had about $140 in all. "That's enough," Campbell said, "I'll sell you a gun for however much money you got on you right now, here today."

Bashnaw thought about it. He hesitated, "Naw, I guess I don't really want to spend my money," Bashnaw ruminated. "I don't want to buy no gun anyhow."

97

Campbell never discouraged Bashnaw. In fact, Campbell continued to encourage Bashnaw to purchase a gun and, alternately, ridiculed him. "Man, you're a chicken, that's all," Campbell taunted. "You don't want to do it. You won't do it even if you get the gun." Bashnaw's girlfriend, Cleland, just listened.

After a while, Bashnaw gave in, "OK. OK, man, so I'll buy your gun. Come on, let's go," Bashnaw slurred. Campbell and Bashnaw stumbled out to Bashnaw's car.

"I knew about Kevin going to buy Campbell's gun," Cleland had stated. Even though she knew of the plan, Cleland did not call anyone. "I just thought Steven was saying about this gun and all just to get Kevin to drive him home," Cleland later explained.

Bashnaw then drove Campbell over to the house of Campbell's parents to get the weapon. The two men were gone about a quarter of an hour.

When Bashnaw and Campbell returned, Cleland saw the .22 caliber, sawed-off Remington rifle and five shells. "You and Steve got to leave now," Bashnaw told Cleland, "because I'm going to kill myself."

Cleland went into the bedroom with Bashnaw. "Don't do it," Cleland pleaded. "Wait a while. Things will get better."

Bashnaw countered, "Why not? What have I got to live for?" And after Bashnaw asked her to, Cleland agreed to keep his dog.

Bashnaw then left Campbell alone in the bedroom to console Cleland, while he found a pen and paper to write his suicide note.

In the bedroom, Campbell and Cleland spoke in very low tones, inaudible to Bashnaw who was still scribbling his farewell message. Cleland asked Campbell, "Those bullets you gave Kevin, were those bullets *really* blanks?"

"Yes, they were blanks," Campbell pretended, "besides, the firing pin doesn't work." In the worst case scenario, Campbell feigned, Bashnaw would get a powder burn.

SLUMPED OVER THE KITCHEN TABLE

"I believed him," Cleland contended, so I agreed to leave with Campbell. The pair did not leave immediately though. They watched Bashnaw place the shells and rifle on the kitchen table. Campbell and Cleland left Bashnaw alone at the kitchen table writing his suicide note. It was sometime between 3:00 or 3:30 in the morning when Campbell and Cleland went out together, leaving Bashnaw behind by himself, with the rifle and his suicide note. When they left, the shells were still on the table. Cleland drove the two of them to Campbell's house. About 4 a.m., Cleland went inside. That night she slept on the couch while Campbell stumbled upstairs to his wife.

Bashnaw's roommate, Alfred Whitcomb, arrived home at approximately 4:00 a.m. The lights were on and Alfred saw the suicide note on the kitchen table. "I've got to find Kevin," Whitcomb thought to himself.

Whitcomb searched the house. Unable to find Bashnaw, Whitcomb figured Bashnaw had left the house. Whitcomb waited up about 20 to 30 minutes longer, but Bashnaw still did not return home. Whitcomb lay down and fell asleep on the couch.

About 11:30 a.m. the next morning, one Billy Sherman arrived at Bashnaw's home, looking for Bashnaw to help repair his motorcycle. Going to the kitchen for coffee, Sherman and Whitcomb found Bashnaw slumped at the kitchen table with the gun in his hand. The unsigned suicide note read:

DR. DEATH

Dear Mom:

I love you but you think I robbed a store. I would never do anything like that.

The county coroner, Dr. Kopp, listed the cause of Bashnaw's death as *suicide*: self-inflicted wound to the left temple. No autopsy was performed. No time of death was even established.

Suffering from a bad case of "the morning after," when Cleland heard the terrible news, she was still at the Campbell house. Glaring at Campbell, she sneered, "Just blanks?"

INCITEMENT TO SUICIDE

"It was a willful, deliberate and premeditated killing," the prosecutor argued, "for Campbell to incite Bashnaw to suicide because Campbell overtly furnished a gun to an intoxicated person, in a state of depression. We agree," the prosecutor went on, "that Michigan has no definition of the term *murder* in its books of statutes. The crime of murder is defined in the common law."

But the appeals court disagreed. "Homicide is the killing of one human being by another," the appellate judge ruled. "The term *suicide* excludes by definition a *homicide*. Simply put, Campbell here did not kill Bashnaw.

"Defendant Campbell had no present intention to kill Bashnaw. No doubt, he provided the weapon and departed. No doubt, he *hoped* Bashnaw would kill himself. But, hope alone, though fulfilled, is not enough to constitute murder," the appellate judges opined.

The common law is an emerging process. The judge who applies the common law, applies the customs, usage and moral values of the present day. "In none of the cases after the 1919 *Roberts* decision has a defen-

100

dant, responsible for incitement to suicide, been found guilty of *murder*," the court observed. "Instead, defendants have been found guilty of lesser crimes."

Yes, *negligent homicide* was the crime in 1979: a Montana court found guilty a defendant who cocked a gun and threw it on the bed during an argument with his drunken wife.

Yes, *manslaughter* was the crime in 1961: a Massachusetts court found guilty a defendant who loaded and gave a gun to his wife who had previously attempted suicide, urged her to shoot herself, called her "chicken," and advised her to take off her shoes when she couldn't reach the trigger.

Yes, *involuntary manslaughter* was the crime in 1980: an Iowa court found guilty a defendant who loaded a gun, clicked the hammer twice to bring a live round into the chamber and then placed the gun within reach of his girlfriend, who was intoxicated and seriously depressed.

In the few cases where incitement to suicide has been held to be a crime, there has been no unanimity as to the severity of the crime.

The court then read from a list, "A number of state legislatures have enacted legislation prohibiting incitement to suicide. These laws may evidence present day social values. Conviction of incitement to suicide is a crime which may bring imprisonment of 15 years (in Florida, Minnesota, or Missouri), or of 10 years (in Arkansas and Oregon), or of 5 years (in Wisconsin), or of 1 year (in Maine). In Colorado, incitement to suicide is treated the same as the crime of manslaughter."

But, Michigan has no law making it a crime to incite someone to commit suicide. Likewise, two-thirds of the states in the United States have, thus far, not held incitement to suicide to be a crime.

It is not clear that incitement to suicide was ever considered murder at common law. Whether incitement to suicide is a crime under the common law is extremely doubtful.

"The court finds no unanimity of custom or usage strong enough to be given the esteemed title of common law," the appeals court said. "Whatever conduct may constitute the crime of incitement to suicide is vague and undefined. No reasonably ascertainable standard of guilt has been set forth."

The appeals court gravely concluded, "The conduct of Defendant Campbell is morally reprehensible; however, his conduct is not criminal under present Michigan law. The remedy for this situation lies in the legislature, not with these courts.

"The trial court is reversed. The case is remanded with instructions to quash the information and warrant. Defendant Campbell is discharged," the court ordered.

POST SCRIPT

Campbell was found not guilty. He only provided the means for Bashnaw to kill himself. Bashnaw made his own decision to commit suicide. The final act belonged to Bashnaw . . . not Campbell.

Though exonerated in the death of Bashnaw, Campbell was arrested at least nine times between 1981 and 1992. He has served time in the county jail in St. Clair, Michigan and the state prison in Jackson, Michigan. By age 34, Campbell was in Missouri serving 20 years for kidnapping and armed robbery.

After reading the *Campbell* case, Kevorkian concluded, "There's no law against assisted suicide in the first place. Even if there were a law on this, assisted suicide would still be justified," Kevorkian reasoned. "I have no fear of the law in this society. But we're still in the Dark Ages in many ways."

chapter seven

Preliminary Exam

A relaxed Kevorkian, 63, appeared in a corporate-grey suit and tie. Joking with admirers, Dr. Death gladly autographed copies of his book, *Prescription: Medicide.*

At the preliminary examination, District Judge James Sheehy first declared the 1920 *Roberts* case, involving the arsenic potion Paris Green, to be irrelevant.

Initially, Sheehy admitted into evidence Kevorkian's homemade video of the gruesome death scene. It was like something out of a Stephen King novel. The judge refused to play the macabre tape in open court.

The assistant prosecutor desperately argued that Wantz just imagined her pain. "The only problem with Wantz is that she had a mental illness and she needed mental health treatment," Bunting persisted.

An involuntary recipient of immunity from prosecution, Marjorie Wantz's husband William, was forced to testify. Conceding his wife could have stopped the suicide even until the last moment, William Wantz testified, "I heard Dr. Kevorkian say, '*You don't have to do this for me. You can stop.*'

"Then I said, '*Marj, you don't have to do this. We can go home.*'

"But she indicated, '*No,*' she wanted to go on," Mr. Wantz narrated.

No eyewitness testified that Kevorkian himself had actually activated the Mercitron or the carbon monoxide gases. In fact, to the contrary, everyone who testified asserted that it was not Kevorkian who triggered the devices but, rather, it was Wantz and Miller themselves.

When death scene witness Janus was asked if it was Miller and Wantz who activated the machines, she asserted, "Absolutely. Absolutely."

And another Bald Mountain eyewitness, Sharon Welsh, declared, "I saw Sherry Miller pull the screwdriver that started the tank of gas." But Judge Sheehy was to err when he chose to ignore this uncontradicted and compelling eyewitness testimony.

VACUUM IN LAW

Judge Sheehy noted the "total vacuum in Michigan law of physician-assisted suicide." The judge even referred to the *Detroit Free Press* poll which overwhelmingly favored physician-assisted suicide.

In the end, Kevorkian smiled impishly as the staunch Catholic judge dogmatically ordered Kevorkian to stand trial for murder. "I wasn't surprised; I expected it," Kevorkian allowed.

A showcase trial was planned. Arrangements were made to hold the expected three-ringed spectacle in a 350 seat auditorium to accommodate the anticipated three-week trial, hosting a global assembly of reporters.

But the plans were short-lived. Nine months after Wantz and Miller died, Circuit Judge David Breck handily dismissed first-degree murder charges against Kevorkian on July 21, 1992.

Citing the 1920 *Roberts* case, judge Breck said that "Dr. Kevorkian's actions and Frank Roberts' actions were distinguishable due to the physician-patient relationship between the two women and Dr. Kevorkian." The jurist wrote in his opinion:

Common logic dictates that if suicide is not a crime (and it is not, in Michigan), then someone who assists should not be criminally responsible.

A person can refuse life sustaining treatment which will cause death, provided the physician is willing to assist and the patient is lucid and meets rational criteria. The distinction between assisted suicide and the withdrawal of life support is a distinction without merit.

The court rejects the medical examiner's definition of homicide, which equates assisted suicide and homicide. The act of a physician assisting a suicide is not a criminal act.

Physician-assisted suicide is not a crime in Michigan, even when the person's condition is not terminal.

Then Judge Breck directed a specific plea to Kevorkian:

You have brought to the world's attention the need to give this topic paramount concern. This judge, however, respectfully requests that

*you forego any other activities in this field,
including counseling, for the time being.*

*To continue, I fear, hurts your cause because
you may force the Legislature to take hasty,
perhaps, improvident action. Give the Michigan Medical Society and the Michigan Bar Association more time to do right.*[51]

SHIRKING DUTIES

As with the dismissal of charges in Janet Adkins'
death, Prosecutor Thompson again appealed the dismissal of these charges. "I feel I would be shirking my
duties if I did not appeal this decision."

· While both relieved and happy at Judge Breck's decision, Kevorkian scoffed at the notion of ceasing to assist
suicides, contending it would be wrong to stop. Challenging the judge, the physician asked rhetorically,
"You're going to watch a person suffer in agony while
somebody's debating?"

"You cannot legislate this," Kevorkian protested.
"You don't need a law and no law can address every
situation." Instead, Kevorkian urged his fellow doctors
to establish procedures for regulating physician-assisted
suicide. "It's the responsibility of organized medicine,"
Kevorkian propounded. "This is a medical service. It
always was."

Two years earlier, Kevorkian had thrown down the
gauntlet, challenging, "If it's legal, let me do it. If it's
illegal, stop me." In reply, the Michigan Legislature
started studying the issue. By now, it was clear that
Kevorkian was not an outlaw. Though, indeed,
Kevorkian remained a law unto himself.

In his final pledge to Judge Breck -- who had unilaterally dismissed murder charges against him -- Kevorkian

conceded, "I will wait . . . but not if the case is extreme."

In summer 1992, when Judge Breck issued his Opinion and Order, Dr. Death was actively counseling several other patients who needed his help in arranging their own exits. Kevorkian was receiving several calls per week from chronically ill people. One patient told Kevorkian: "I have lost all dignity. If you could put me on your list, I would appreciate it."

chapter eight
The Fifth Commandment

Before multiple sclerosis (MS) affected her, Susan Weaver Williams' life was common fare. She planted petunias, met friends at the K-Mart coffee shop and set about on her cosmetics route as an Avon Lady. With her eyesight failing her, she rode an Amigo scooter about town and her sister Mary Neubert would chide, "God, would you slow that thing down."

She spoiled her son, Danny, hooked rugs and played bingo. On Sundays, she and Danny would bicycle to Guardian Angels church for 10:30 mass.

For the past 12 years, Williams also had been fighting a losing battle with MS. Across the United States, hundreds of thousands of people are afflicted by MS precipitated when nerve coverings over the brain and spinal cord deteriorate. While most MS patients live normal lifespans, less than five percent die from the disease.

As a youngster, Williams was the frail child. "She was sick all of her life," Neubert noted. As a baby, Williams had skin problems, eczema: "I'd wake up in the middle of the night and hear her scratching herself with a comb or brush," reflected sister Nancy Vervaras. "I don't ever think she slept the night through."

As a teenager, Williams had 13 surgeries for a malignant tumor on her forehead; 10 operations more were needed to reconstruct her eyebrows and eyelid. "I just remember she always had a big bandage around her head," Neubert recalled. Williams also suffered from rheumatic fever, a heart murmur, asthma and allergies.

One year older than Susan Williams' father and 30 years his wife's senior, Leslie Williams was her good-natured husband. When they started dating, Susan Williams was 18 and Les was 48. She married Les the day she turned 21. But that was then and by now, Les had retired from his work as a bowling alley manager. "Les was the cat's meow," Neubert says. "He was super."

As a young mother, Williams was hospitalized for two months with a heart lining infection. After a bout with cancer, she became legally blind at about age 30 and needed reconstructive surgery on her left eye. Despite her debilities, Williams struggled daily to put on her make-up and look her best.

In 1980, while she was struggling to cope with her blindness, MS had begun its torturous process of crippling her. Williams' hands were tingly and shaky while her legs were numb and she was imbalanced. Within two years, she could no longer ride the scooter. In two more years, Susan Williams needed help to walk. Les filled a shopping basket with bricks for ballast; it got his wife to the mall each morning.

At the early stages of MS, from one day to the next, Williams knew not how she would feel or even if she might walk the next day. Besides the advancing MS, she suffered from other diseases, was incontinent and endured a bleeding skin condition.

112

The Fifth Commandment

When MS struck, Williams couldn't walk, write her name, go to the bathroom or brush her teeth unassisted. Now in his late 70's, Les would have to shoulder his wife off to bed like a Raggedy Ann doll.

In winters past, with his wife sentenced to an electric wheel chair, Leslie would scout along the sidewalk, shoveling the snow ahead of her pathway as they trekked to the corner K-Mart.

Tearful phone calls had summoned police from the blue-collar suburb of Clawson to the South Marias Street home four times in the last year because Williams had fallen and 81 year old Leslie could not lift her up again. Decades earlier, Williams's mother had chastised her saying, "You're crazy to marry him. He'll probably end up in a wheelchair with you having to take care of him." Ironically it turned out the other way around.

"She was in bad, bad shape," said one neighbor. Her friend, Barbara Ferguson, affirmed, "She was determined to beat this. She didn't give up until the last."

It is the hard cases that are used to justify euthanasia. Danny, now 30, brusquely described his mother's day, from start to finish:

> *In the morning, my dad would get her up, take her out of bed, put her in a wheelchair, wheel her out to the dining-room table. She would have coffee, a cigarette, whatever. They would listen to the radio, my dad would do whatever he had to do and at around 2 o'clock in the afternoon, the radio would be turned off, the TV would come on.*

> *Dad would fix dinner at around 6, then he would have to feed her. And then they would watch TV until about 10 o'clock and then he would put on her salve, for her skin, head to*

113

*toe, front to back and this took until about
11:30. Then he put her to bed.*

*And it went on, day after day, Monday
through Sunday.*

For some time, when Williams needed to go to the
bathroom, Les would carry her from the wheelchair to
the toilet and pull down her pants. But then she became incontinent, requiring a catheter.

Nurses were hired to bathe her. Nonetheless,
cellulitis attacked her skin and the smell of her body
would precede her. "It's like Sue was trapped inside
this rotting body," her sister Joanne Gibbons realizes.
"All I could think of was, she's inside there somewhere."

CRY FOR HELP

"At the beginning, Sue's faith was very strong," recounts Neubert. "Sue just felt she was going to conquer
this and that somehow this was God's plan. But finally
she got to the point where, you know, she would just
say, '*Why me?*'"

In February 1992, Williams asked Gibbons, "What
would you think if I told you I wanted to commit suicide?" Later, Williams asked Gibbons to write a letter
for her to Kevorkian. She did so in March.

"I wrote it because she wanted me to," Gibbons reports. "I thought, well, maybe she'll change her mind.
I didn't really think she was going to go ahead at that
point. Or that Dr. Kevorkian would either. He was in
legal trouble already so, I thought, no way."

Kevorkian already had been mandated not to assist in
suicides under three separate court orders as well as
under conditions in a bond by which he was released
from jail. Free on bond, defendant Kevorkian was await-

ing a murder trial in the deaths of Sherry Miller and Marjorie Wantz.

Within two days, Dr. Death called and a meeting was arranged. He agreed to counsel her and aid "in the sense of being compassionate, being present at the time of her death." At first, Kevorkian did not think Williams was ready. So he undertook several videotaped counseling sessions to help Williams clarify her own thinking on ending her life.

Williams's sister Nan was supportive proclaiming, "The medical profession has just gotten to where they can keep you alive forever, but they don't know what to do with you." Like other family members, husband Les was initially reserved until he relented by conceding, "If she wanted me to stand on my head and jump off of a building . . . I'd do it."

TALK OF GOD

In one of many counseling sessions over nearly a three month period, Kevorkian confronted Williams' Catholicism, reminding her that the Archbishop of Detroit, Bishop Adam Maida, had branded as a sin what Kevorkian was doing. In turn, Williams' sisters, Mary Neubert and Barbara Smith, professed their doctrinaire Christianity saying, "I believe it's a sin 'cause that's the way I was brought up. It's the only unforgivable sin in the Bible." But Williams's husband Les and son Dan disagreed flatly, "I don't think its a sin."

Ultimately, it was Williams who would determine her own fate. Was Williams fearful -- if she confessed to Kevorkian a belief that suicide was a sin or that she would be condemned to hell -- that Kevorkian would refuse to assist her? Williams said, "I don't think God's gonna approve of it. I think He won't approve of it. . .

But I don't believe I will go to hell. I think I'm going to heaven, but I'll never see God."

RELIGIOUS CONSULT

With religion playing such a powerful part of these discussions, Kevorkian asked Williams to consult with a priest, Fr. Robert B. McGrath.

On April 8, 1992, Catholic priest McGrath, a friend of the family, instructed Williams for some two hours. The priest's own mother had died of multiple sclerosis. No doubt, Fr. McGrath preached nothing of the goodness of planned death. Instead, he certainly reminded Williams of the Fifth Commandment: *Thou Shalt Not Kill.*

Certainly, Fr. McGrath may have thought to invoke some of the words his religious superior, Archbishop Adam Maida, who had preached:

> *Every moment of life is precious, from the first moment of conception until the last natural breath. In that process, even suffering -- yes, even terminal suffering -- has value and meaning.*
>
> *Anyone who has watched a loved one slowly fading from this world knows how deeply touching those last hours can be. Love is purified, memories are healed and new meaning and hope are given to the survivor.*
>
> *Honor the importance of allowing someone to die . . . according to the timetable of God . . . . To shorten that process . . . . by ourselves . . . . is morally unacceptable. It is not our right or privilege to intervene in the mystery of our own . . . . tenure on Earth. . . .*

After counseling with Williams, Fr. McGrath wrote, "Sue is being asked to go through with something that she has always been taught is wrong." But that enraged Williams all the more. "I think Fr. McGrath took everything out of proportion," Williams said. "I talked to him because I had to." Some would agree with Williams:[52]

Dear Editor:

I think this whole thing about Dr. Kevorkian is pathetic. If you want to commit suicide with the help of a doctor, that's your own business and no one else's.

The only people who are against [physician-assisted suicide] are people who don't think you have a right to your own life -- and religious wackos and morons.

KEVORKIAN CONTINUES COUNSELING

Despite the corporeal work of mercy by Father-confessor McGrath, it was obitiatrist Kevorkian who counseled Williams. After her priest gave up and before she died, Kevorkian met with Williams five times from early March to mid-May. Kevorkian did attempt to dissuade this long-sufferer from her design to kill herself.

Fr. McGrath criticized Kevorkian for "taking advantage of Sue Williams . . . The nature of her debilitating disease makes her vulnerable to any bizarre idea that comes along. Fascination with this bizarre plan has clouded her love and concern for her family."

Kevorkian countered, however, by saying "Organized medicine is to blame for every medical crisis. It is dominated by religious ethics."

In time, Williams announced, "I have decided to go ahead and end my life."

DR. DEATH

Despite the nickname he had earned, Dr. Death had counseled Williams against her plan. Williams explained that "Dr. Kevorkian has counseled me not to do this until I was absolutely sure this was what I wanted. I am happy to have his assistance to help me since I am unable to do this myself." Indeed, Susan Weaver Williams was a very stubborn lady and it was difficult to sway her once she made up her mind.

PHYSICIAN DIAGNOSIS

The ebb and flow of life and death is often interrupted by startling arrays of technology which snatch dying patients from the jaws of death. This course of suffering reaches out and withdraws unendingly, like the cursed fruits that teased and tortured King Tantalus. The joy of life erodes until its course runs into a hideous torture of mind and soul where the living die by inches.

In February 1992, some three months before Williams passed on, physician Lawrence Eilender of Bingham Farms, Michigan had written a letter (February 26, 1992) indicating that Williams required a wheelchair, wore a permanent catheter and suffered skin infections. There was no chance of the MS going into remission. Since 1980, Dr. Eilender wrote, Williams' multiple sclerosis had. . . .

> . . .*showed no improvement with steroid therapy in the past. At the present time, there is no hope for reversal of her neurologic condition.*

But when Eilender was asked to fill out some forms affecting Williams' suicide, he refused, telling Kevorkian, "I don't want to have anything to do with you."

118

The Fifth Commandment

DRESS REHEARSAL

In videotapes of the half dozen meetings with Williams before she died, there were eerie rehearsals of Williams putting on and taking off her gas mask. "She has trouble putting it on, so someone will have to help her put it on," Kevorkian said during one trial run. Indeed, she would need practice.

In those videotaped sessions, there were also rational discussions. Williams was apprehensive at the onslaught of the coming summer heat which always worsened her situation. She questioned details about upcoming events: How long would it take before she lost consciousness? What would happen to her body? Could she trust that the carbon monoxide mixture she breathed would actually kill her?

Williams might not have known that Kevorkian had written that he was a ". . .champion [of] execution the way it was sometimes done in ancient Greece and Rome, with carbon monoxide. That colorless, odorless, tasteless and supremely soporific gas is far superior to all other conventional methods and offers most of the advantages of thiopental without requiring any medical intervention whatsoever not to mention even an enhanced post-mortem bloom in the complexion of light-skinned corpses."[53]

During the more than two hours of videotaped discussions with Kevorkian, Williams would practice putting on and breathing through the gas mask, demonstrating that despite her MS, she could do the task herself without anyone's assistance. A small mechanical timepiece with a brass ball whirled in the background. Kevorkian was both nervous and excited.

Janus shot the videotape. Williams struggles uselessly to move her legs and one arm; finally, she barely manages to lift a cup of coffee. In the video, she responds in slow, slurred speech:

Kevorkian: Do you feel all right?

Williams: Fine.

Kevorkian: She's not a candidate for lethal injection because her veins are too poor. . . .We could inject you through the jugular, but it looks kind of gruesome with a needle stuck deep in the neck. You wouldn't want a needle in your neck vein, would you?

Williams: No. I wouldn't.

Kevorkian: Sue, put it in plain English: What do you really want?

Williams: I want to die, really, in plain English. I'm tired of sitting and watching the day go in and out. I do the same thing every day. I just sit at the table all day. I don't get dressed anymore.

Kevorkian: Well, people would say that's rather, to put it mildly, extraordinary.

Williams: No. I'm tired of sitting and seeing the day go in and out.

Kevorkian: You won't back down?

Williams: No way. I want to get out of here.

FINAL PRAYER

May 15 was set as the day when Williams would make her final exit. Grandchildren, nieces and nephews were brought for visits they did not know were final. Williams was in a lighter mood, though consumed with minutia about her cremation, how the neighbors would react, memorial services.

Williams' multiple sclerosis was so advanced that she could not write and could only scrawl an illegible *X* as her signature. On May 14, the day before she took her leave from this Earth, Williams dictated a suicide letter which read in part:

> *To Whom it May Concern*
>
> *I've never had a remission from multiple sclerosis since first diagnosed in 1980. It has been downhill ever since. I don't want to live in this condition any longer ... I have the right to end my own life.*
>
> *The quality of my life is just existing -- not living. The only time I was able to leave my home in the last year or so was to go to the doctor and I can't even do that anymore. I am completely incapacitated and am unable to do anything for myself.*
>
> *I intend to pull a lever to activate the release of carbon monoxide and nitrogen and I pray that Dr. Kevorkian will be exonerated of any wrongdoing in this case. I am so thankful he was able to help me.*
>
> *Sincerely yours,*
>
> *X*

DR. DEATH

The letter, signed with Williams' *X,* was witnessed by her sisters (Nancy Vervaras and Joanne Gibbons) and nieces (Meghan K. and Mary F. Gibbons).

A PEACEFUL STREET

On Friday, May 15, Leslie Williams dutifully canceled the Meals on Wheels food service for his wife.

Williams' sisters arrived on that Friday morning. Sister Barbara Smith communicated a futile message from her husband: "Tell her I said to cut the shit out and forget about this." But Williams was adamant responding, "No way! I'm ready."

On that Friday, Kevorkian sat quietly in the orderly bungalow on South Marias Street. Outside, spring was in blossom, birds chirped and it was a gorgeous sunny day. It couldn't have been more peaceful.

Inside, Williams, 52, would soon lie motionless. In her tiny rear bedroom, she rested on her back, protected by the railing in her hospital-like bed. A poem called "Motherhood" was written on a plaque hanging on the wall. Clothed in a nightgown, flowered sheets draped her bed. Williams had kept her appointment with a visiting nurse so she would look respectable. Everything was just the way she wanted it.

At her left hand, tied to the bed railing with a piece of twine, was a tank of carbon monoxide. The gas was used in industrial and automotive systems tests and no license was needed to purchase carbon monoxide. Kevorkian did not buy the carbon monoxide.

The tank was a customized device with a nine inch, homemade metal handle screwed onto the valve that controls the gas flow with an off-on valve. From the mouth of the tank snaked a plastic tube which transported the poison from the gas container to a mask that Williams would place over her mouth. The makeshift

122

handle allowed Williams to use her good hand to activate the fatal mixture of carbon monoxide and nitrogen. Kevorkian jury-rigged the device which dispassionately dispensed the poison gas.

WOMAN'S LAST THOUGHT

While death stood patiently at her doorstep in Clawson, Michigan, Williams was not thinking of herself. Deanna Seifert, 10, had disappeared from a slumber party one week earlier in the Detroit suburb of Warren, Michigan. It was national news, capturing everyone's attention for days.

Everyone feared the worst about little Deanna, brooding that she had been kidnapped, but for weeks no one knew what actually had happened. Everyone was worried about Deanna . . . and, even in her final moments, so was Williams.

Calmly and unemotionally, Williams had one final question of her only child, 29-year-old Dan. Williams quietly asked, "Have they found that little girl yet?"

"I don't know if the Seiferts care," young Dan Williams recounted, "but the last person my mom was thinking of was their little girl. But that was my mom for you. She was always worried about other people, especially little children. She wanted to take care of everybody -- she just couldn't."

It was mid-morning when it came time to don the mask and pull the ill-fated handle. Williams raised her wobbly left hand to draw the plastic mask over her face. A hissing sound was all that could be detected, escaping from the nearby tank.

On May 15, 1992, Williams took charge of her life as it dictated the terms of her death. While she extinguished her life with a veil of carbon monoxide gas, Kevorkian watched as though a sentinel.

Within two minutes her breathing deepened and in four minutes her complexion became red, her eyes widening. At one point, Williams asked why it was taking so long. To Kevorkian, she whispered her final words, "Goodbye and thank you." Falling unconscious, her eyes closed somewhat. Her breathing became stertorous, gradually diminishing in volume and frequency. She began to gasp deeply. At 10:10 a.m. she died.

POLICE ARRIVE

"I didn't have any problems being there," Dan Williams later recalled, "but after my mom was gone, after it happened, then I started to get nervous. I got pains in my stomach and I felt pretty sick. My hands were sweaty and I remember shaking: I didn't want to be in the house. Not at all."

About 10:27 a.m., Dan dialed *911* to report a suicide to the Clawson Police Department. Someone -- among those present -- had told Dan what to say. When the police dispatcher asked for details, he did not give his or his mother's names. The dispatcher thought Dan Williams sounded "evasive and pretty guarded. He seemed to be very selective in what he said."

Lieutenant Daniel Zalewski said that, when police arrived, Williams had no detectable pulse or breathing. Officers lifted her mask covering her face and nose to perform artificial respiration. Perhaps, a minute later, the hissing sound stopped as the tank emptied its lethal contents. About 15 minutes later, Williams was pronounced dead by a doctor.

ATTENDING PHYSICIAN

When officers had arrived, Kevorkian was sitting silently in the kitchen. Regarding the doctor's presence at the death scene, Oakland County Prosecutor Richard Thompson demanded to know, ". . .What was he doing in the house?"

Kevorkian says he was there because his only concern is to alleviate suffering and because helping patients end their suffering is a logical extension of the care that compassionate doctors should offer. "I know that sounds Pollyanna-ish, but it's not," Kevorkian submitted. "It's not because I'm overly compassionate, because there are more compassionate doctors than me. It's because I have an overriding sense of duty . . . a physician's obligation is what drives me -- nothing else. And that's why I ignore everything else, including intimidation."

But, Kevorkian was not alone at the Williams' home. Keeping vigil at the bedside were a half dozen others, including Dan, Williams' four sisters (Smith, Neubert, Gibbons and Vervaras), as well as Janus.

Eighty-one-year-old Leslie Williams was aware of his wife's decision. Because Leslie was in poor health, it would have been too much strain for him to attend his wife's suicide. Leslie felt compelled to stay with relatives during his wife's last moments . . . out of fear that authorities would harass him if he remained at Williams' side when she made her exit.

One newspaper reader was concerned about being isolated at one's death bed and wrote:[54]

Dear Editor:

. . . All over the world, hospitals are crowded with people enduring incurable pain. And our government thinks Dr. Kevorkian is wrong for trying to help people who want to die with dignity.

125

DR. DEATH

People should be able to die with their loved ones around if they want, and not have to worry about the consequences their loved ones will have to face afterward.

SCENE OF THE CRIME

Medical examiner Dr. Ljubisa J. Dragovic was summoned to the Williams' home. He describes the scene as follows:

> *I was appalled. They made a mockery of a death scene. Kevorkian's attorney Fieger was offering me coffee. They were serving pizza. They were watching television. It was like a party. It was grotesque.*

> *I don't understand how they can say they are providing a service. To me, it's a disservice to humanity. I was disgusted.*

Under the possibility of arrest, Kevorkian continued to threaten that, if jailed, he would begin a hunger strike and starve himself to death. Volunteering to turn himself in to authorities if required, Kevorkian was permitted by Clawson Police to leave the Williams home after their investigation concluded.

THE SUICIDE STATE

Michigan Governor John Engler did not know Williams while she was alive. But when he heard news of her death, he demanded that the Michigan Legislature act speedily to make physician-assisted suicide illegal. Obligingly, legislators joined in a stampede to stop Kevorkian in his tracks.

"[The Governor] is very disturbed by Kevorkian's actions," cautioned John Truscott, Governor John Engler's spokesman. "He doesn't want Michigan to be known as The Suicide State."

But Kevorkian did not sit idly by: "The Pope runs the State, not [Governor John] Engler," Kevorkian taunted, castigating the Michigan legal system (that had so doggedly prosecuted him) as "a resurgence of the Inquisition."

In turn, Fieger portrayed the Governor as a "dumbbell" and a "truly goofy, stupid man, certifiably evil" for demanding legislation outlawing doctor-assisted suicides. "[Engler's] an unlikable guy," Fieger blazoned. "He looks like [Governor Michael] Dukakis without the helmet on."

AN INVISIBLE MAN

The medical examiner was true to form. There were three valves on the apparatus. All three must have been opened for the deadly carbon monoxide to be released.

Valve #1 released gas from the tank. Valve #2 controlled the gauges and measured the flow. Indeed, valves #1 and #2 had been opened by someone other than Williams.

Valve #3 controlled the flow of gas being released. With valve #3 closed, it didn't matter that valves #1 and #2 were open because the deadly gas could not escape. Without Williams opening value #3, she would not have succumbed.

The coroner investigated the manner and cause of death, but not who was involved. Accordingly, the coroner ruminated that someone -- other than Williams -- opened valves #1 and #2 on that tank to permit the flow of carbon monoxide. "I came to the conclusion that [Susan Williams] could not have done everything by herself," decided Deputy Chief Medical Examiner Dr. Kanu Virani, who went on to say:

> *The reason for it is the active participation involved. Someone brought the [carbon monoxide] canister into the house. Someone tied it to the bed. Someone connected the face mask. Someone opened the two valves on the canister and modified a third valve so it took a minimum of effort to open it.*
>
> *There is no question in my mind [Susan Williams] wanted to die. But she could only pull up the mask and open the third valve. The rest of the things other persons had to do, whether it was one person or many persons. That makes it a homicide.*

Though this was a death caused by self-administered carbon-monoxide, undoubtedly, Williams needed help to administer the lethal gas she inhaled: so the coroner's final ruling was *homicide*. "It's up to the police," Medical Examiner Dragovic proclaimed, "to determine and identify the perpetrator and to determine whether there was a conspiracy with more than one person helping to carry out the death."

Kevorkian's attorney did not miss a beat in discrediting the medical examiners as "lunatics" who were "indulging in the fantasy that an *invisible man* snuck in there and took Williams by the arm and killed her."

The next step in the police investigation would be to prove who killed Susan Williams. As with the Wantz and Miller deaths during that fateful night on Bald Mountain, none of the witnesses to Williams' death were talking with the Clawson Police.

The Fifth Commandment

With two pending murder charges against Kevorkian, Prosecutor Thompson was doubtful about bringing another criminal complaint. "We don't know whether there is sufficient evidence upon which to base any action," Thompson cautioned.

Fieger chastised Prosecutor Thompson, alleging the prosecutor "will do anything and make up any lies to try Kevorkian again. The entire populace of Oakland County should remove Thompson from office. He should be tarred and feathered and run out on a rail."

In fact, no charges were ever brought against Kevorkian in the death of Susan Williams.

chapter nine
Sufferer's Last Wish

Though his Michigan medical license was suspended in November 1991, Kevorkian issued a challenge to the medical profession: "I invite them to observe; maybe they can learn something. I think if they came along with me, visiting patients and going from start to finish, their perceptions would change."

Kevorkian offered to, "Put a group together -- a judge, a philosopher, a garbage collector, and a house-wife -- and have the whole group be with me, right there to the end. Watch me like a hawk."

Dr. Death even urged Prosecutor Thompson to grant immunity from prosecution for anyone who attends a Kevorkian suicide. Prosecutor Thompson rejected that suggestion out of hand, saying, "That's preposterous."

In an attempt to stir the medical profession to action, Kevorkian conferred with members of the Michigan State Medical Society and its Bioethics Committee. But after a 30 minute meeting, the Society rejected his plea to name a panel to evaluate patients seeking Kevorkian's treatment.

Kevorkian had confronted the "emotional obstinancy" of the medical establishment before, charging ". . .the medical profession is psychically (philosophically) retarded, drifting aimlessly without a coherent or even workable ethical code and blissfully forsaking any semblance of ethical autonomy. . . ."

Kevorkian had predicted, "It is to be expected that the medical establishment will thwart attempts to implement the practice [of physician-assisted suicide] for *ethical* reasons. Physicians tend to be conformist by instinct and training and would, therefore, shun as ostensibly immoral anything not sanctified by prevailing public opinion or pending legislation."

Kevorkian has urged that, "The medical profession must take the lead immediately to [eradicate] this last unjustified taboo [against medicide] by elevating the most important life event -- called *death* -- to the place of honor in the hierarchy of ethics it has always deserved."

Rather than join Kevorkian's crusade, the Society was treading water by calling for "a self-imposed moratorium on any physician-assisted suicide in Michigan until there is a public consensus on the issue." Kevorkian was incensed that "the medical profession continues its futile hair-splitting of platitudes in the face of inexorably changing taboos."

"While you're blabbing and flapping your gums, people are dying," Kevorkian indignantly charged. "I've held off with a couple of cases. I can't hold off much longer. I'm going to proceed." Ten days later, Kevorkian did proceed, as promised.

One letter to the editor distinguished Kevorkian from some physicians:[55]

Sufferer's Last Wish

Dear Editor:

I am certainly in favor of Dr. Kevorkian. He is the only doctor who really helps people. The others just want your money. And when the money is gone, the person remains suffering.

So he is an angel, absolutely an angel.

"He has defended his position around the world." Fieger predicted, "He's not going to talk anymore. He's just going to go ahead and act."

At that time, obitiatrist Kevorkian was counseling four people on assisted suicide and had three others on his waiting list.

AN UNINVITED GUEST

His medical license suspended and with three criminal appeals pending against him, Kevorkian would again dispense his own unique version of mercy. His fifth patient was to be a woman, like the others so far.

The suicide of Lois F. Hawes, 52, did not emerge from transitory despair, or youthful anxiety, or medically-treatable depression. Hawes was a victim of terminal cancer; her lungs had been ravaged long before she had lost all hope.

"She used to be outside in her yard all the time," neighbor Mike Sobocinsky related. "She'd be there fixing it up. It was her pet project. But she didn't come out much this summer. You could tell her illness was weighing heavily on her."

Hawes had discussed her plans with her family. She knew her actions eventually would become public. But the reality was that she could no longer stand the pain.

With the approval of her doctors and family, at 10:45 a.m. on Saturday, September 26, 1992, Hawes pulled a mask over her face: she, herself, activated the flow from a canister of carbon monoxide on a machine which Dr. Death had invented.

With the legal authority to dispense prescription drugs suspended along with his medical license, Kevorkian now employed carbon monoxide instead of the Mercitron, which had made him famous.

Kevorkian, then 63, had supplied the carbon monoxide Hawes inhaled and was present when she made her final exit. "Please give me the gas," Hawes pleaded before she pulled the lever that invited the lethal property into her despoiled lungs.

When she departed, Hawes' sons William and Robert were at her side, along with two sisters and a niece. Divorced, her ex-husband was uninvited. This contingency of family members had gathered at the Waterford Township, Michigan home of Neal Nicol.

For Hawes, there was no better option. Though death was an uninvited guest, it refused to leave. Hawes confronted interminable humiliation, unremitting pain and escalating physical and mental deterioration. She was tormented by the burden she had unwillingly forced upon her loved ones. She concluded that to exit now was her best alternative.

Hawes "was sicker than you can ever imagine. All she wanted to do was end the pain and end her life," Fieger explained. "Anybody who thinks she didn't have the right to do this is either *ignorant* or a *lunatic*."

DOCTORS CONCUR

Unlike Kevorkian's previous four patients whose suicides he assisted, Hawes' own physician was completely cooperative.

In the days before she died, Hawes made a videotape naming the physicians who had cooperated in her decision to end her own life. Hawes' treating doctors "understood the serious nature of her condition, understood she was mentally competent and didn't try to interfere," Fieger reported.

Her treating physician knew she planned suicide. Before agreeing to assist, Kevorkian reviewed Hawes' medical reports, X-rays and CAT scans. Hawes' treating physicians not only had shared these medical records with Kevorkian but they had actually met with the obitiatrist.

Hawes also was psychiatrically evaluated, at Kevorkian's request. After that session, the consulting psychiatrist told Kevorkian that Hawes' "mental competence was not a problem," said Feiger.

The police who arrived at the death scene were extremely polite and compassionate. Sergeant Rick Grigger of the Waterford Township Police Department promised that an investigation was underway.

WOMEN AND SUICIDE

While Kevorkian has counseled some men, his patients who had died thus far were all female. Hawes was the fifth woman to have died with Kevorkian's assistance, suggesting a concentration of female patients.

While fewer women than men actually *commit* suicide, women actually are more likely to *attempt* suicide. Yet for every woman who actually kills herself, there are four men who commit suicide. Caucasians are twice as likely to commit suicide than Afro-Americans.

Of the more than 250 million people in the United States, some 30,000 suicides are reported annually. That means about 80 people daily are reported to have killed themselves. Yet, some say that -- since many fatal "accidents" are actually suicides -- the statistics on suicide are underreported.

With the death of Hawes, some of Kevorkian's critics had suggested his suicide house calls were the work of a "serial mercy killer," branding Dr. Death as "an ethical outlaw, a free-lance death dealer providing paraphernalia and know-how" to the ill women upon whom he preyed.

But Fieger defended his client saying "He's been portrayed as morose and a killer and it's important that the national press . . . do not see him as a lone wolf helping people commit suicide."

A HOSTILE MILIEU

In Hawes' death, Kevorkian purposefully selected the venue where he practiced medicide -- Oakland County, Michigan -- even though Hawes had lived in adjacent Macomb County, Michigan.

This choice of venue was somewhat perplexing because authorities in the neighboring county of Macomb had been quoted in the press as openly supporting Kevorkian.

Macomb County Medical Examiner Werner U. Spitz, M.D., had distinguished Kevorkian's actions, publicly stating, "I'd call them suicides because these are people who, whatever they did, they did it to themselves." Dr. Spitz is a nationally renowned forensic pathologist who concluded: "If [Kevorkian] pulled the switch, that's one thing. But he didn't!"

In stark contrast, Dr. Spitz's counterpart in Oakland County had consistently ruled that Kevorkian's physician-assisted suicide was *homicide*. Invariably in Hawes' death, Oakland County Coroner Dr. Ljubisa Dragovic, as if the Mephisto, steadfastly held that her death had constituted a homicide saying, "The moment there is someone there, actively helping, it's not a suicide anymore."

Not only did the Macomb County Coroner seem favorably disposed toward Kevorkian, but so did Macomb County Prosecutor Carl Marlinga. In plain contrast to his neighboring prosecutor in Oakland County, Marlinga did not necessarily oppose medicide as practiced by Kevorkian. Marlinga practically invited the obitiatrist to set up an obitiatry clinic in Macomb County when he said, "If [Kevorkian] set everything up and did **not** pull the switch . . . I think that the presumption would be: No, it would not be murder under that exact circumstance," Marlinga opined.

So, it was quite possible that Obitiatrist Kevorkian might soon practice medicide freely and without fear of criminal prosecution -- with one step over the county line.

Strangely enough, Kevorkian did not accept the invitation to a safe haven in bordering Macomb County. Elevating the importance of public opinion, Kevorkian elected to remain in the midst of upheaval. "We feel very comfortable in Oakland County," Kevorkian's attorney explained. "We know the majority of the people in Oakland County support us."

A MARTYR FOR MEDICIDE

All said and done, there was something of the martyr in Kevorkian. To cross the county line might have precluded his prosecution . . . and consequently would have diminished some of the national publicity for his cause. For to remain in Oakland County was Kevorkian's self-fulfilling prophesy, not to mention guarantee, that he would be slaughtered as the sacrificial lamb for his prescription: medicide. The writings of Kevorkian offer a clue:

The enormous pressure of acute human need
is what forced (and is still forcing) the issues,

137

*often beginning with the terrible personal sacrifices of now revered "heretics." The promulgation of planned death is still more risky, because even though conventional morality is now in a bewildering state of flux, the **martyrdom** of those who transgress these obstructive and far more serious laws entails the culpable homicide of murder. Therefore, in spite of a growing demand for it in our "enlightened" time, a rational program of planned death will be more difficult to espouse and to debate and indeed impossible to implement in such a hostile milieu [emphasis added].*

Remember it was Kevorkian who had vowed that, if authorities jailed him, he would undertake a hunger-strike, starving himself to death.

NOTHING OUTLAWING SUICIDE

Again, as with Susan Williams, Oakland County Prosecutor Richard Thompson planned to bring no criminal charges against Kevorkian, as Michigan had no law preventing suicide. But some state legislators were furious about the statutory void. "There's no stopping Kevorkian unless we pass legislation that literally will take him off the streets," railed Michigan State Senator Fred Dillingham, R-Fowlerville.

Prosecutor Thompson was flummoxed. Every time he had levied criminal charges against Kevorkian, some judge would come along and dismiss those charges. There was no law in Michigan at the time outlawing physician-assisted suicide.

The Michigan Court of Appeals was still figuring out what to do about Prosecutor Thompson's three appeals of the dismissal of his criminal charges against Kevorkian in the planned deaths of Janet Adkins, Sherry Miller and Marjorie Wantz.

While the great wheel of justice whirled round in the state appeals court, the Michigan legislature was simultaneously spinning its wheels.

"Shame on them," Thompson charged. "Their inaction is disgraceful. It's been more than two years and they don't have the guts to take a stand. The Michigan Legislature has become the laughing stock of the country because of their inaction," Thompson decried. "They have made Michigan the only state that has legalized euthanasia. They have created a void . . . and Kevorkian has filled that void."

FINGER POINTING

But Michigan State Representative H. Lynn Jondahl, D-Okemos, who chaired the House Committee on Death and Dying, defended his legislative colleagues: "All of us are wishing that we knew how to resolve the issue, but that's more difficult than some have suggested." Jondahl labored mightily for two years, only to bring forth not a single recommendation!

To add party politics and personalities to the brew, republican Dillingham was quick to chide democrat Jondahl charging, "Michigan is becoming known internationally as a suicide haven and it just sickens me. I don't know how long Lynn Jondahl needs to digest something, but while he's at it, Kevorkian is getting away with murder. People have more protection under consumer laws than they do if . . . [Doctor Death is] around." There really was no middle ground on this issue.

But observer Margaret L. Betts of Birmingham, Michigan was miffed by the moniker conferred upon

Kevorkian asking, "Why do the media continue to label Kevorkian *Dr. Death*? We're all going to die. The choices are life with quality death with dignity -- or, I hope, both!"[56]

IMMORALITY AND THE LAW

To some, Kevorkian was a murderer while to others he was a trail blazer. "When they call me a pioneer, they're wrong," Kevorkian explained. "I'm a person at the right time when the mores are changing."

"The Nuremberg tribunal said, '*The first thing you do is check the morality of the law and, if it's immoral, you disobey it*,' " Kevorkian proclaimed. "You pass any law against assisted suicide and euthanasia and I will disobey it . . . because it is immoral medically. When the law itself is intrinsically immoral, there is a greater duty to violate the law."

Kevorkian was then counseling a handful of patients who were suffering from cancer, emphysema and severe arthritis which he described as "fatal illnesses."

Helping someone commit suicide is a felony in some two dozen states.* Yet, doctors have helped patients in agony kill themselves for decades. Patients in severe pain with no hope of relief often obtain from their own treating physician a generous supply of sleeping pills or pain killers to commit suicide.

"There are lots of doctors who have seen patients in a horrible condition," said another of Kevorkian's attorneys, Michael Alan Schwartz who practices law with Fieger. Treating physicians wink to patients in feigned warning, saying "Here are some pain pills. Don't take all of them at once." The physicians know an overdose is fatal. So does the patient.

---

* See TABLE A , page 245.

140

chapter ten
The Last Straw

Tucked away in Moon Township, 12 miles west of Pittsburgh, 45-year-old Catherine Andreyev learned of her terminal cancer in December 1991.

In 1986, at age 39, surgeons performed a modified radical mastectomy removing one breast. But cancer had spread to a lymph node.

By 1988, surgeons removed part of her left lung.

In 1991, the disease had ravaged both lungs and had metasticized to her breast bone and then elsewhere in her body. The doctors said it was cancer, *The Big C.* But, after two years of chemotherapy, Andreyev elected to discontinue treatments.

"What?" she thought, "so I can lose my hair, turn orange and be sick most of the time?" She wanted to let the disease take its course. To her, that was common sense. Her friends were supportive, never insisting she undergo this therapy or that treatment. "What good is quantity when you can't have quality?" she would ask.

BEST FRIENDS

Andreyev met her friend, Diane Collins, while both were teaching at a Montessori preschool in Allison Park, Pennsylvania. Andreyev who was an only child, had no children, had never married, and taught at the Montessori school for a decade.

Andreyev loved music, particularly the symphony. Flute and piano were her instruments. She sang soprano in the choir. Andreyev was a potter who had crafted the miniature harps which decorated her home.

As a member of the Audubon Society, she went bird watching in the west and camped in Pennsylvania's natural areas. "She really appreciated life and nature and was always interested in children," reported her friend, Diane Flannery, 39, of Mars, Pennsylvania.

Before giving birth to Andreyev in New York City, her mother, Zonia Porter Andreyev, was a stage actress in the 1920's and 1930's. When she was but two, her father, Alexis Andreyev -- a musician by trade and a Latvian by birth -- died. In time, Andreyev's mother became a teacher.

Andreyev attended Miami University of Ohio, a small liberal arts college. The auburn-haired student was well-read and her graduate work was as a reading specialist.

By 1986, she had joined Coldwell-Banker's *Million Dollar Club* as a successful real estate agent. But in 1992, cancer forced Andreyev to quit her real estate job.

By May 1992, Andreyev was compelled to quit her post as a reading tutor. "She wanted to enjoy this summer because she knew it would be her last," recalled Collins, her closest friend for 20 years.

A PLEA FOR HELP

It was during that 1992 summer that Andreyev raised the subject of physician-assisted suicide with Collins

142

sharing with her a brochure from The Hemlock Society U.S.A.

Andreyev remembered all too well her own mother's slow, agonizing death two years earlier: rigged with tubes; her tongue swollen; breathing from a pipe protruding from her trachea; a painful cancer death accompanied by a fair amount of thrashing. Andreyev vowed that she would not go that way.

Andreyev knew what would be in store for her if she chose to live. Her life would be consumed by a slow and agonizing death. Her bones would become so fragile that they would break when she would be turned in bed. She would lie undignified and uncomfortable for 20 or 30 minutes in her own excrement until hospital staff became available to change her bed pan. The pain medication would never last long enough, nor do as much as it was supposed to do. She would slip away, dying by inches. She likely would lose her hair to chemotherapy and would weigh half of her normal self. After months of sheer agony, she may die alone in a hospital bed. But these were her worst fears, a nightmare to be avoided by hastening her own death.

To Andreyev, her dilemma was either to endure abysmal pain or to stumble around so drugged-up that she would barely resemble her former self. She counseled with her dearest friend, Collins. "I found a way to end my pain," she advised Collins. "Can I count on you for help to commit suicide?"

"No, absolutely not!" Collins retorted. "I will do anything possible to make sure that you are comfortable. You have lots of love. But I will have nothing to do with your suicide." There was no mention between them of Kevorkian then, or ever.

In Pennsylvania, assisting suicide is a felony, punishable by ten years in prison and a $25,000 fine. Yet, at that time, assisted suicide had not yet become a crime in Michigan.

LOOKING FOR HEMLOCK

It was The Hemlock Society of Michigan that helped Andreyev make contact with Kevorkian. Andreyev had telephoned Janet Good, president of The Hemlock Society of Michigan, with 200 members. Andreyev suffered intractable pain and wept over the telephone.

"She was so obviously in constant pain," Good recalled with a lump in her throat. "I felt so sorry for her, so empathetic. She was really, really at the end of her rope. I remember how upset I was. She was so young," Good vividly recalls.

Good gave the telephone number of Kevorkian to Andreyev who initially contacted the doctor by letter. Early September was the first occasion when Andreyev spoke with Dr. Death by phone.

DYING BY INCHES

In the last few months of her life, Collins was watching her friend, Andreyev, deteriorate. She could not walk without help; her daily life had become a torture of excruciating pain; her breathing was so labored that she could only sleep sitting up. But death's outrage sometimes pales next to a body kept alive by tubes and wires.

"Each and every day for her was a day of horror and dread and she wished to end that. . .," confided Michael Alan Schwartz, Kevorkian's attorney and law partner with Fieger.

Some patients either lack funds or are not considered near enough to death to qualify for hospice assistance. When patients do qualify, a hospice offers a

144

quality environment for the dying process. Yet, a hospice can do little for patients with intractable pain.

In the end, though, a nurse from the hospice program was assigned to visit Andreyev every few days. Without prolonging agony, hospices focuses on *care* and not necessarily *cure*; helping to manage pain and other symptoms, usually at home and with family members' participation. Nonetheless, most hospice patients leave its care by dying.

SHE GOT A *TICKET TO RIDE*

On Saturday evening, November 21, 1992, Andreyev was taking transdermal morphine via an arm patch to block the pain. She was in pain, walking with difficulty around her home, eating spaghetti with red sauce. Her friend Collins was there.

"She was not bedridden. She was ambulatory and she could have been made more comfortable," Collins reported. "She was nowhere near maxed out on what the doctors could have done for her pain."

But by Sunday, without a *goodbye*, Andreyev had departed in her car with another friend, Betty Ouzts, Moon Township, Pennsylvania, for an arduous six hour car trip from Pennsylvania to Michigan. The trip had been advanced by ten days because Andreyev feared she was becoming too weak to travel to Michigan. Along the way, she was forced to stop three times to take intervenous medications to stymie the pain in her right hand and arm. This was her gift from the cancer that was killing her by inches.

When finally arriving in metropolitan Detroit on Sunday night, though in great pain, she was equally in great spirits. Andreyev was finally happy to take the last few steps toward the final peace of a death that awaited her. She had traveled straight into the arms of the man who, to some, was the ghoulish Dr. Death, the *bete noire* of pathology, the mad monster of medicide; but to Andreyev that Sunday night, Kevorkian was *Dr. Life*.

Kevorkian first met his patient, Andreyev, that Sunday night when she arrived in metropolitan Detroit. "Imagine, in her condition, in the kind of pain she was in, traveling by car," Kevorkian pondered. "It shows how much she wanted this."

Andreyev's oncologist knew of her planned death and had prepared a summary of her condition. Kevorkian had consulted with Andreyev's physician and reviewed her medical records. It would be with Kevorkian's help that she would consumate her death wish.

THE MISSING LINK

It wasn't until 8:00 a.m. Monday that Collins noticed Andreyev's car was missing. But summoning the police by then was like running to slam the barn door shut. . hours after the horse had run away.

When the Moon Township, Pennsylvania police arrived, Collins was handed a goodbye note, scribbled by Andreyev and entrusted to a neighbor for delivery. Her By this stage, her once beautifully scripted handwriting had deteriorated into childlike scrawl. On two sheets of yellow legal paper torn from a thin pad, Andreyev had penciled a note to Collins:

Dear Diane:

Thank you for all your love and care. I know you would disagree with this decision. Please forgive this and understand this.

Catherine

By the time Collins had read this farewell, Andreyev was being accompanied by Kevorkian in Michigan to the home of Neal Nicol. As a medical technologist, years ago, Nicol helped Kevorkian in the experiments transfusing blood from dead donors into living patients.

Nicol's home -- where Andreyev died -- was exactly where Hawes had ended her life with Kevorkian in attendance less than two months earlier.

Down the street, neighbor Cornelia Van Huizen, 78, had lived in this quiet Waterford Township lake community for more than a half century. Nicol had surveyed his neighbors about whether they had any objections to allowing Kevorkian to use his house. "We didn't," Van Huizen said. "Oh, I guess it's [Nicol's] business what he does there, but I sure wouldn't mind if it didn't happen there quite so often."

BEDSIDE MANNER

Andreyev's friend, Dorothy Shorsher, 71, of Tiffin, Ohio was with Andreyev in the Nicol home. "We all tried to get her to change her mind. But she had her mind set on what she wanted to do. It was her decision and no one else's. I hope people will understand there is a need for people to have a choice when there is no other way out."

Also nearby her were friends Leslie DePietro, Ann Arbor, Michigan, and Ouzts. Andreyev hugged and kissed her friends goodbye then rested her head on a pillow while Shorsher went to wait in the kitchen.

Shortly after noon on Monday, Andreyev donned a Kevorkian face mask to breathe deeply the pithy blend of carbon monoxide and nitrogen. She pressed a lever, releasing the gases from a small canister near her feet -- a tank supplied by Kevorkian. In a little more than a minute, she was deeply asleep; ten minutes later, she had found her final peace. Andreyev died about 12:30 p.m.

DePietro, 50, had befriended Andreyev 30 years ago. "Catherine made the right choice. But I was probably not prepared for the impact it had on me. I was praying and I kept telling myself she would be with God soon."

ROUTINE INVESTIGATION

By now, medicide had become routine in Oakland County, Michigan. The investigation was cursory and completed in short order. Within an hour, Andreyev's body had been whisked off to the Oakland County Medical Examiner's office.

Dr. Dragovic's autopsy indicated extensive cancer in her lungs, liver, lymph node and bones. The coroner ruled her death a homicide, just as he had ruled in each of Kevorkian's five previous assisted-suicides.

A still stinging Oakland County Prosecutor, Richard Thompson, branded Andreyev's death an "embarrassment to the state of Michigan." In the past, Thompson has likened Kevorkian to "Jeffrey Dahmer in a lab coat." Dahmer was the Chicago murderer who cannibalized his victims.

But the physician was unimpressed. "Dick Thompson is irrelevant to this, just as he would be to a brain surgery or a kidney transplant or any other medical procedure," Kevorkian deadpanned.

After Andreyev's death, Kevorkian declared that medicide is ". . . now an accepted medical specialty. Period. Now, the medical profession should come forward and say that medicide is now an acceptable medical service, as it does with every medical specialty." Kevorkian had coined the term *medicide* because he dislikes the phrase "physician-assisted suicide."

"This is very simple," Kevorkian defended, "I consider this a legitimate medical service."

But Andreyev's best friend, Collins, left behind in Moon Township, Pennsylvania, was unequivocal and unrestrained in her denunciation: "Dr. Kevorkian took advantage of a woman in depression," Collins lashed out angrily. "Instead of alleviating her pain, he took her life."

LAWMAKERS ACT

With the death of Andreyev, Kevorkian had willingly handed his detractors the weapon they needed to whip up a ban against medicide. The death of Andreyev was the straw that broke the legislature's back.

"You cannot legislate this," Kevorkian chided lawmakers. "Every case is unique. This cannot be legislated. That's what's wrong with all these silly initiatives. No other medical practice has law controlling it. It's the medical profession's fault that this is happening."

Kevorkian contended, "The only state law needed for the proposed practice [of medicide] is one which makes assisting any suicide a felony for everybody except obitiatrists."

All of this fell on deaf ears. The general alarm was sounded: "There's no stopping Kevorkian unless we pass legislation that will literally take him off the streets," warned Senator Dillingham.

The very next day, the Michigan House of Representatives passed a bill (72-29) which outlawed assisting suicides. The Michigan Senate later adopted the bill (24-6). It was to become a felony, punishable by up to four years in prison and a $2,000 fine; it would become a crime to provide the physical means, or to participate in a physical act, that helps someone commit suicide. In 1985 under a similar Texas law, a woman was fined for helping someone else address and stuff envelopes with suicide notes to friends and relatives.

"Who do these legislators think they are? Do they think they are free to use the power of government to tell someone -- afflicted with a terminal disease -- that they have not suffered enough yet to earn the right to die?" asked attorney Howard Simon of the ACLU. "This new law is wrong and callous."

"I would hope the elected representatives of Michigan would send a clear signal to Jack Kevorkian," Representative Joe Palamara, R-Wyandotte, shallowly implored. "Hit the road, Jack, and don't you come back no more."

But Senator Jack Faxon, D-Farmington Hills, was heard complaining that the legislature was being bamboozled into passing an unconstitutional bill of attainder -- a criminal law aimed at one individual. "It's absurd. You don't write legislation prohibiting one man from doing one thing."

Senator John Kelly, D-Grosse Pointe Woods, ranted and raved about Kevorkian being a "psychopath" and warning of "this sicko" who is "going around willy-nilly killing people" and of the doctor who "takes women in their mid-50's . . . and terminates their lives."

As tempers flared in the legislative debate and reached the boiling point, Senator John Welborn, R-Kalamazoo, raised a call to arms, proclaiming it was time to crush "Jack the Ripper."

Placing the debate in context, Kevorkian said, "I have never cared about anything but the welfare of the patient in front of me. I don't care about the law. I don't care about injunctions. I don't care about legislators."

Attorney Michael Alan Schwartz called the medicide ban an act of "barbarism and unenlightenment. This was an obvious and unfortunate reaction to the fact that Kevorkian helped [Catherine Andreyev] a very ill

woman. This is a political vendetta . . . a personal vendetta now. . . .This is just base vindictiveness. People
in Michigan want the option to choose," Schwartz reasoned. "This bill takes away that right."

But one *Detroit Free Press* letter to the editor implored the legislature:

VOTE
ON KEVORKIAN

*I wish someone would start a petition so we
could get this on the ballot and let everybody
vote on it. Because I think the majority wold
want this. And the self-righteous politicians
can go back and talk to themselves.*

The new law was not scheduled to take effect, however, until four months later -- on April Fool's Day.

STAGE IS SET FOR FUN

"The stage is set for fun," Kevorkian proclaimed.
"They don't realize the dumb mistake they've made."

But would Kevorkian continue practicing medicide
once the law took effect? He was fierce and uncompromising: "Law has no business in medicine. Law is irrelevant to me; I am held to a higher standard," Kevorkian
insisted. "I'm a doctor. All I care about is the suffering
patient who needs help."

Kevorkian was pressed to say if he would continue to
counsel patients about suicide when the ban became
law. "It's an immoral law and I will not obey an immoral law," he warned. "No law should keep a doctor
from serving the best interests of his patients."

But would Kevorkian break the law after it went into
effect in Michigan? "No law should keep a doctor from
serving the best interests of the patient."

"I will help a suffering human being at the right time when the patient's condition warrants it, despite anything else. That's what a doctor should do," Kevorkian declared.

"Several of my patients are close, but none are imminent," explained Kevorkian. "There's nothing more to say. If you don't believe me, call my bluff," Kevorkian tested. "Nobody calls my bluff."

Did Kevorkian fear being jailed for assisting suicide contrary to law? "Well, I've been [in jail] twice and I wasn't frightened. When you walk down the aisle with holding cells on each side and someone spots you and then there's suddenly an uproar of cheers and hands come through the bars to shake your hand, would you worry? That happened both times."

chapter eleven
Winter Solstice

"**I** wonder what Catherine Andreyev had," Marguerite Tate wondered aloud after Andreyev succumbed to death's demand. Tate lived in Auburn Hills, Michigan and suffered from ALS (amyotrophic lateral sclerosis). Statistically, she would die in three years. Some call it Lou Gehrig's disease, named after the baseball great who perished from this motor neuron ailment. ALS victims slowly surrender their ability to move or speak; the brain's message never reaches their muscles. Death visits when the diaphragm no longer makes the body breathe.

"I wish Dr. Kevorkian would help me," Tate declared. As the living, she envied the dead. She had first talked of suicide after her ALS was diagnosed in 1990.

Similarly, another woman, Sue Rodriguez, 42, from Victoria, British Colombia also suffers from Lou Gehrig's disease. Though terminally ill, the Canadian courts had denied Rodriguez the right to medicide. She appealed that ruling which was based on a Canadian law making assisted suicide a felony, punishable by up to 14 years in prison.

In a photograph taken decades earlier, Tate appeared like the sturdy farm woman in the classic painting, *American Gothic*. But now, at age 70, suffering from a degenerative and fatal disease, she would protest: "I don't think Dr. Kevorkian knows how bad I am. I can't even wash my face. I'm like a baby," she slurred.

Those were the words she spoke — when she still could speak. It wasn't long afterward that her voice was gone. Then, she could only utter downcast pleas through her electronic voice synthesizer.

But as recently as November 1992, Kevorkian still was encouraging Tate to live. She wrote, "I was ready to give up a long time ago, yet Dr. Kevorkian keeps telling me that I am not ready to die."

Indeed, Kevorkian may have followed Tate for a year or more, with five or six counseling sessions. Kevorkian could see over these sessions how she had deteriorated. It was a medical problem that he would have to evaluate.

Kevorkian insisted she see a specialist at the ALS clinic at Detroit's Henry Ford Hospital for an evaluation. Kevorkian wanted to know if there was something more that could be done to alleviate Tate's pain. She dutifully went, hoping to persuade Kevorkian to accept her as a patient.

While doctors offered Tate nerve blocks and exercises, her pain was incessant and tormenting. "I'm waiting for the report. I want to show it to Kevorkian," she said, though she had no formal doctor-patient relationship then with the physician.

Not long ago, Tate could still drive her car to the local McDonald's for coffee; now, however, the only ride she could take was in her wheelchair -- from room to room. Home-bound, her intellectual diet consisted of TV game shows. She was under nearly constant care.

Since July 1992, Tate's neighbor, Marion Sherill, 72, a Baptist preacher, could only offer her grim ministrations, vegetables and scripture readings. Yet the preacher came not to lecture but to listen. "Marguerite told me that she had talked with Dr. Kevorkian. Of course, I wanted her to reconsider, but I didn't feel it was my place to try to counsel her."

"You have to understand how it was for her. It just wasn't working," confided her friend, Garvin Mosser, age 71, White Lake Township, Michigan. Tate was divorced and she had dated Mosser back in the late thirties; they had been close friends for 50 years.

"If she wanted to take a pill, she'd have to use her finger to shove it down her throat," Mosser explained. "She couldn't go to the bathroom by herself. None of her muscles were working. It wasn't any kind of a life for her."

If you asked, Tate would have shown you her new toy -- an overly-wide computer keyboard that served as a voice machine. The mechanism produced a strained hiss and swish when she tried to speak her mind. Tate would first type then, after an interminable quiet, the machine would speak as Tate's proxy saying, "I want to go as soon as possible."

MARCELLA LAWRENCE

Hearing of the Michigan legislature's new law which would soon ban assisted suicide, Marcella Lawrence scoffed, "I wish these legislators could have my pain for just one night."

At 67, Lawrence had to carry a scorecard with her itemizing all of her ailments. Her list included osteoporosis, emphysema, heart problems, ulcers, cirrhosis of the liver and arthritis in her elbows and knees.

Living alone in a Clinton Township, Michigan apartment complex, Lawrence told friends of her designs in the summer of 1992. It was her choice. Even if someone had tried to dissuade her, it wouldn't have done any good anyway. Friends said that Lawrence "was real stubborn, real set in her ways."

Lawrence was a retired registered practical nurse. She had worked in nursing homes and hospitals in metropolitan Detroit. Her maladies finally prevailed, forcing her to quit work.

"I can't go shopping in the supermarket. I haven't played bingo in a year. I'm losing my sight," Lawrence chronicled. But she refused to go to any more doctors. "All of the doctors seem to think I should continue to try this and try that and I should go here and go there. I can't . . . I refuse to force myself anymore! I suffer too much."

More than death itself, she feared failing in an *unassisted* suicide, ending up in a vegetative state, withering away in some nursing home. Pressed to her limits, Lawrence promised, "If I was up on the 23rd floor, I think I'd jump. I have no fear -- I feel like I've led a good life . . . and I'm ready to meet my Maker."

Since summer ended, Lawrence had met with Kevorkian four times imploring his help. "The truth is, it's very difficult to get Dr. Kevorkian to help you," Lawrence complained. "He often thinks that it is not time for you and that you have not exhausted every means to help yourself."

There was no disputing the meaning of Lawrence's statement. "Yes. I make patients suffer," Kevorkian admits. "But they do it for me because they trust me and they know the option is there. They know they're not going to die in extreme agony. I keep them going as long as possible."

156

DECEMBER NEWS CONFERENCE

On December 3, 1992, there was a news conference. Tate, in her wheel chair, and Lawrence, seated, joined Kevorkian for a press photo opportunity. He stooped down in between the two women. Before reporters, Tate and Lawrence criticized passage of Michigan's law prohibiting assisted suicide.

These two ladies announced they were ready to die, but each wanted Kevorkian's assistance. He stated that the two women ". . .were ready months ago, but I've been the one saying you've got to go on." The obitiatrist had been insisting that each see specialists.

To the oft-heard criticism that Kevorkian preyed upon women and that no male patient of his had yet committed suicide, the obitiatrist explained that "Women are far more realistic about facing death than men . . . and women have the guts to do it."

Desperate to end their lives sooner, the impending suicide ban was accelerating everyone's timetable. A frenetic pace would result as the doctor worked to beat the legislature's April Fool's deadline. Prospective patients were panicking: "They're going to shut Dr. Kevorkian down April 1 . . . but I'm going to be on one of the lifeboats off the Titanic," one prospect predicted. "The luxury of having more time is gone."

Tate had been publicly sharing her wish to die for almost a year and to do so with Kevorkian's aid. She had joined the doctor on the TV program *Donahue* to express her views.

Lawrence wanted to end her life before the holidays. "People who feel like their life is not worth living any more should have the right to die," Lawrence told the press. "I'm afraid if I do it myself, I may botch it up and I'll be left a vegetable for my daughter to take care of."

DR. DEATH

AN OPEN LETTER

On December 11, 1992, one week before she hastened her death, Lawrence addressed a letter to the residents of the state of Michigan:

To the Residents of Michigan:

I am hoping that Dr. Kevorkian will be with me in my final hour . . . . However, if he refuses, I will end my own life. I can't go on like this any longer. My life has no quality, it isn't even a good existence. ...I can no longer go to the grocery store ... or even cook. A meal which used to take me two hours to prepare now takes me two days, as I am unable to stand long enough to even cut an onion . . . .

. . . Dr. Kevorkian keeps telling me that I am not ready to die. My regular doctor has . . . sent me to a pain clinic. If my pain was in one place in my body, they might be able to help me by giving me a nerve block. But the pain is in too many places.

The Michigan legislature is making a big mistake. I certainly hope that they never have to watch a member of their family suffer in severe excruciating pain!

It is doctors like Dr. Kevorkian who can help a person die with dignity, which is every person's right! . . . The people of Michigan who support Dr. Kevorkian need to march in protest . . . and make their voices heard!

Winter Solstice

Just remember always -- But for the Grace of God -- YOU could be walking in my shoes!

Marcella Lawrence

DOUBLE INDEMNITY

The date for the double suicide of Tate and Lawrence had been set far in advance. It was Tuesday, December 15, 1992, just one week before the winter solstice -- the shortest day of winter. At 10:45 a.m. in Tate's home, Kevorkian assisted in another double suicide.

Though Tate's relatives knew that she would be committing suicide, none attended the event. Tate was divorced and was fiercely independent, rarely relying on others. She wanted to die in her own home.

Tate, draped in a blue nightgown, rested in her living room on the brown Stratolounger. As Garvin Mosser sat with Tate at the end, she would give him simple gestures, special signals, trying to keep *his* spirits up, smiling about the good old times they shared together. Mosser held Tate's hand and the two of them sorted through photos of her parents. Also there supporting Tate was another friend, Ester Wright. Speechless from her disease, Tate waved and smiled *goodbye* to her friends as they took their leave, walking from the room.

Then, Kevorkian was all set to go. The obitiatrist was assisted by Janus and Nicol. In the front bedroom of Tate's home was Lawrence with her daughter, Jo Ann Allen of Mansfield, Ohio and a friend, Joanne Dobberowsky of St. Clair Shores, Michigan. Both Tate and Lawrence died when they inhaled carbon monoxide through masks -- all part of a machine invented by Kevorkian.

"I was just tore up inside. Just tore up," Mosser reflected. "I can't believe Tate's gone. I still have her notes in my pocket but I can't look at them," Mosser explained. "Maybe someday I will."

chapter twelve

This Time, It's a Man

The telephone rings every day at Kevorkian's Royal Oak walk-up apartment. He is accessible. He answers the telephone himself. A steadily increasing stream of prospective patients seek him out.

"Five people got a hold of me today. Two letters and three phone calls," Kevorkian reported. People call from all over the country.

"I have many requests from other states. I have two more in Michigan. One in New York. One in Indiana. All of these are medically justified," noted Kevorkian.

"In the last couple of months, I've been averaging two or three a day. Of course, I can't hardly help all of them because they have to follow the procedure. The procedure is so complicated, sometimes it annoys me. But I have to follow it," Kevorkian vowed. In any event, "You act only after it is absolutely justifiable," Kevorkian exhorts. "The patient must be mentally competent, the disease incurable."

161

While the uninitiated clamor for laws and guidelines, there is nothing impetuous about the involvement of Kevorkian with a suicide candidate. "It's well-tested, well-planned and a well-executed medical procedure," he stated. "And I consider myself a specialist in this area."

Before the obitiatrist will assist in a suicide, Kevorkian requires elaborate medical and psychiatric examinations. He deplored his detractors saying, "They just criticize. . . .With all the harassment and obstacles thrown in my way . . . I've done it correctly." Kevorkian argues that he always tries to dissuade people from committing suicide.

But certain conditions produce such mental anguish that suicide may be defended. For example, "You can't dope up a quadriplegic," argues Kevorkian. "There's no pain to alleviate, but the mental anguish in the head is immense, especially after five or ten years of lying on your back looking up at the ceiling."

Kevorkian challenges his critics to debate: "I will argue with them if they will allow themselves to be strapped to a wheelchair for 72 hours so they can't move and they are catheterized and they are placed on the toilet and fed and bathed. Then they can sit in a chair and debate with me."

THE PROCEDURE

The Procedure developed by Dr. Kevorkian is elaborate and applies to all of his medicide patients. "The criteria is not somebody having a bad day," Fieger defends. "It's somebody having a tremendously horrible life as a result of their disease." *The Procedure* includes:

3 Insisting the patient clearly and repeatedly requests suicide over an extended period of time;

3 Persuading patients to prolong their lives by further treatment with specialists, including pain medication;

3 Demanding a clinical diagnosis of an incurable, terminal illness (or that the patient suffers from severe, unrelenting, unmanageable, incurable pain without hope of medical improvement);

3 Confirming a patient's diagnosis with their treating physician and assuring that the course of treatment has been proper with all medical options exhausted and unsuccessful;

3 Requiring the patient be mentally competent and, if necessary, evaluated by a psychiatrist;

3 Engaging in videotaped death counseling with the patient and family for several sessions; patients must have full support of their families and everyone must participate in a counseling session on the morning of the medicide;

3 Allowing the patient to choose where, when and with whom the medicide will occur, if possible;

3 Having the patient make an informed and knowing consent, signing waivers, properly witnessed by disinterested third parties and notarized;

3 Guaranteeing each patient the interminable and irrevocable right to reverse their decision at any point, even at the last minute; verifying that a patient's consent remains firm and unwavering; at the slightest hint of "any degree of ambivalence, hesitancy, or outright doubt with regard to the original decision, the entire process is stopped immediately and [the

patient] is no longer -- and can never again be -- a candidate for medicide";

3 Requiring that the patient alone activate the switch which starts the lethal drugs terminating life; and

3 Recording all of this on an official obitiatry form, signed by the attending obitiatrist.

Upon reflection, Kevorkian contends that "The system I've devised has so many controls built [in] that it's almost impossible for abuses to occur. Of course, you're always going to have a crook or two." Remember, Kevorkian says ". . .concepts don't corrupt; humans do."

ALLOWING A TRANQUIL EXIT

From personal experience, Kevorkian has learned that mere knowledge on the part of a dying person that assistance in suicide will be available, indeed, can ease that patient's natural passage:

> *In at least three cases of terminal cancer, I have consulted with the patients, their families, their medical records and their personal physicians and, in all three, the patients proceeded to die with surprising serenity and calm resignation before medicide could be performed.*

Among the reasons for their departure from life before medicide could be performed was that. . .

> *. . .the patients' mental outlook was so relieved of panic after my initial consultation with them that they contentedly made plans*

to fulfill certain personal obligations which had previously seemed inconsequential or burdensome. In this tranquil frame of mind, each of the three patients died naturally within a period of from two to four weeks.

The surviving wife of one such patient, who died of liver cancer which widely metasticized to his brain without ever taking his life, poured forth her gratitude in a letter to Kevorkian writing:

I am sorry the law [politics] doesn't understand what you do for those who need your service and compassion. My husband . . . was in severe pain. . . . After your talking to [him] that night he agreed to get more radiation [but] was never strong enough to get in for treatment. And after your visit, he never talked about talking his life again. . . . We never know what's in store for us. Thank you for caring.

Kevorkian argues that "there will be diminished demand for medicide among patients whose mental panic will . . . be dissipated by the existence of this option."

A FEW DAYS TO LIVE

The Procedure was employed with Jack Miller, 53, once a tree-trimmer. Though a private man, Jack was a wonderful guy, very neighborly, very helpful. Miller lived in a green and white house trailer in the Huron Estates trailer park in Huron Township, in Wayne County, Michigan.

His terminal diagnosis came in September 1992. "He had a bad backache not long ago," one neighbor recalled. "Next thing we know, he was diagnosed with bone cancer. The last time I saw him outside, he was going through chemotherapy and had lost about all his hair."

Miller's disease was reminiscent of a defining event in Kevorkian's life -- his own mother's death:

> *My Mother suffered from cancer, spread all over. Every bone was riddled with it. Can you imagine a toothache in every bone in your body? She was in great agony.*

Just after Christmas 1992, doctors told Miller he had but a few days to live, though he had already been in contact with Kevorkian. By then, Miller was emaciated and was bombarded with big bumps all over his body.

HOSPICE PATIENT

Miller's daily medications were legion, including narcotics, nerve pain medication, a muscle relaxant, an anti-inflammatory drug and more even drugs to counter the adverse side-effects of all these pain killers. The variety of ten different pills -- some of them "horse" pills which doctors prescribed for his pain -- was difficult medicine for Miller to swallow. So, one physician nonchalantly instructed Miller to start taking the medication anally.

Pain is controllable in 90 percent of patients with oral morphine. "The medical professional can't have it both ways. They can't condemn Dr. Kevorkian for doing what he's doing and then sentence people like me to live in hell," thought Miller

Some doctors don't prescribe controlled substances for pain and, when they do, the dosage is insufficient. As a result, pain is undertreated. Physicians stop short of fully medicating pain, knowing that may hasten death.

Their mistake may be in postponing death, rather than concluding life comfortably.

Miller was an outpatient of Hospice of Southeastern Michigan in Southfield. Neighbors also helped. Two brothers of Miller came daily. Cynthia Coffey would rush home from her job as a florist. But even with Hospice, there were lapses in care. Hospice staff would supervise the daily administration of his medications. But his unrelenting pain was not relieved by any of these drugs.

Patients sometimes speak of suicide with hospice staff. "But when they see the hospice program, they don't want to talk about dying, they talk about living," advised Barbara Lewis, speaking for Hospice. "We are able to help almost all of our patients control their pain." Hospice officially opposes medicide. In Jack Miller's case, Hospice's "comfort care" was too little, too late. Miller had to beg for a morphine patch.

For most patients, hospice care works very well; however, even the best medicine cannot assure a comfortable death. Despite the most advanced techniques available in pain management, some people still live and die with pain. Miller stood at the front of that line.

Perhaps, Dr. Howard A. Brody was describing the "Jack Millers" of the world when he said, "The public in Michigan does not have faith that they will receive truly compassionate and effective care. They fear they will be hooked up to a machine, they fear they will be in pain, they fear their wishes will be ignored and that they will be treated as a piece of meat."

FEELING DESPERATION

Like other Kevorkian patients, however, Miller began feeling desperation that the upcoming April 1 ban on assisting suicide would prevent Kevorkian from helping him. In November 1992, Miller had planned to shoot himself. Miller pledged, "I'm leaving - my soul can't take this beating any more." Yet Jack was constrained by thoughts of the mess and the neighbor children. He decided, instead, to call Dr. Death.

In December 1992, after the suicide ban was passed by the Michigan legislature, Coffey, 37, contacted Kevorkian. When Coffey asked Miller what he thought of turning to Dr. Death, Miller said, "Nobody else is helping us." Kevorkian asked her to enclose medical documentation of Miller's problems. The obitiatrist then evaluated the records, going over them with his assistant, Neal Nicol, a medical technologist.

After Kevorkian's review of Miller's case, the obitiatrist suggested a morphine pump or morphine patches, palliative measures never offered before. The Hospice doctor smiled a wry grin and sneered, "Well, it seems like you've been talking to someone." But when Miller demanded morphine, the Hospice physician called him "a charity case." "Kevorkian has more *doctor* in his little finger than other physicians do in their whole body," Coffey said.

Kevorkian visited the home of Miller with his two assistants, Nicol and Janus, for more input. Miller, if he wished, could have friends and relatives present. The visit would be videotaped and, later, summarized in writing.

Miller's case was typical, though there was just one major session. As with many cancer patients, it was obvious Miller was dying. Indeed Miller would wake up mornings asking, "Why didn't I die last night?" One day of suffering in the life of a cancer patient was longer than 100 normal days for someone healthy.

PENULTIMATE PAIN MEDICATION

To some, Kevorkian's crusade might seem macabre. Others tend to dismiss the doctor as a psychopath. But Kevorkian says, "Anyone who does this is going to have an image problem. If I were Satan and I was helping a suffering person end his life, would that make a difference?"

Miller's clamor for medicide did not arise in a vacuum. Pain worsened over time. Choking, Miller could not turn unaided. Miller could not wear a diaper as it hurt his bones and skin too much. Every day, there were messes to be cleaned up. Physicians had been unable to do something as basic as keep him comfortable. His doctor's failure to relieve Miller's pain was a serious breach of faith. It was as important to treat his pain as to treat any other symptom.

While pain relievers made Miller comfortable, they also depressed his vital signs. As death drew nearer for Miller, his organ functions were increasingly impaired as his pain medication increased. In short, to relieve his pain would hasten the end of life. That was necessary in the humane care that Miller needed. If Miller's pain had been managed differently, he may not have sought out the services of Dr. Death.

For Miller and Coffey, there was Kevorkian's death counseling; waivers and consent forms were signed. At a different time and place, *Jack the Tree-Trimmer* might have engaged *Jack the Doctor* in philosophic debate asking, "Under what circumstances can a patient choose death?" Or . . . "What responsibility does a physician have to maintain life where the patient suffers overwhelmingly?" Or . . . "What responsibility does a doctor have to accelerate the process of dying?" But Miller had no time left for debate and, thus, in strict terms, *The Procedure* was followed by Dr. Kevorkian.

On January 21, 1993, Miller was positioned in the hospital bed that had been moved into his mobile home. Only Coffey was at his side, even though Miller's brothers and sisters apparently knew of his suicide plans.

Also assisting was Nicol, Kevorkian's friend and colleague, who aided the obitiatrist in *The Procedure*. Like brother, like sister -- Janus, Kevorkian's 66 year old sibling, was also by his side, as she had been at each of the previous deadly house calls.

Though once a secretary at Chrysler Corporation, Janus had no medical training and provided no substantive assistance. She just sees eye to eye with her brother and feels the way Miller felt -- suffering human beings have rights over their own bodies.

At 8:30 a.m., Miller, otherwise with just days to live, instead, chose to die. On the day of his medicide, the sun glared in his eyes. Miller donned his facemask. "You look like an airplane pilot," Coffey chuckled. Miller laughed and removed the mask. Together they had one last cigarette, puffing so hard. Then it was time.

Miller died simply by tugging on a string tied to his pointer finger on one end and to a big paper clip on the other. The paper clip pinched a tube through which carbon monoxide and nitrogen flowed from a tank brought along by the doctor. The gases streamed into a Kevorkian-designed facemask that Miller wore over his nose and mouth.

Whoever said, "There shouldn't be any such thing as death"? Just as it becomes desirable at some point for a sleepy man to sleep, so too, it now became desirable for Miller to die.

COMMON COMPLAINTS

Medical care for the chronically-ill Miller had a staggering price tag, both in money and emotional costs. While Miller did not fear death, he also did not believe that the duration of human suffering should depend on how much money a patient has to pay. Human torment should not be prolonged merely because insurance will cover the cost of delaying the inevitable.

Miller was aware of some of the abuses of institutional medicine: rarely being involved in treatment decisions; overtreatment of a terminal illness, even when there was no chance of recovery and death was considered imminent; doctors and nurses who ignore a patient's wishes despite soaring health care costs. And if there is any narcotic abuse in caring for the dying patient, it is the *undertreatment of pain.*

Miller's last days were not as comfortable or as pain-free as good medicine and humane care demand. Miller had tumbled into the enormous abyss which separates abstract principles of medicine from the messy reality of caring for a cancer patient.

A FIRST FOR KEVORKIAN

Kevorkian heralds that, "The time has come to smash the last irrational and most fearsome taboo of planned death and thereby to open the floodgates of equally momentous benefit for humankind."[57]

"The time has come to let medicide extend a comforting hand to those slipping into the Valley of Death and to let obitiatry extract from their ebbing vitality the power to illuminate some of its darkest recesses. . . ."[58]

Miller knew he was history in the making: he was Kevorkian's *first* male suicide patient and the *first* to die outside of Oakland County, Michigan.

Reacting to the previous criticism of Kevorkian, Miller's death showed that Kevorkian "isn't just out to victimize women," contended Cheryl Smith, attorney for The Hemlock Societ U.S.A. in Eugene, Oregon.

UNINVITED RELATIVES

While Wayne County Medical Examiner Dr. Bader Cassin had ruled the death of Jack Elmer Miller as a *suicide*, rumblings of discontent began to arise some three months later from the surviving son, Jack Miller,

Jr. The younger Miller refused to believe that it was his father who had pulled the clip which released the carbon monoxide gas.

The younger Miller contended that his father "could only move his arm a little bit and that was it. The rest of him, he couldn't even move at all. There's no way," Jack Miller, Jr. argued, that his father could have committed suicide.

Testifying to television reporters, Huron Township Police Sergeant John Maier offered his own opinion saying that the elder Miller "just didn't look strong enough to pull the clip" on the carbon monoxide tank.

But the distraught son had no personal knowledge of what happened in his father's final moments because he had not been invited to attend; only Coffey, was there. Indeed, the elder Miller feared that if his son knew of the medicide plans, the junior Miller would intervene to stop the suicide.

Huron Township Chief of Police James Caygill complained, "We have questions too, based on what Kevorkian said happened and what we saw. But how can we go any further when we can't talk to the players? Fieger is telling everybody not to talk to us."

Frustrated, Chief Caygill grumbled that Miller's family "had questions about it and, quite frankly, with the limited amount of cooperation we've had from the people present, we're not able to answer those questions. The questions that the Miller family raised are questions that I have some doubts about, too."

Chief Caygill admitted that "What bothers me is the family was not there; but the girlfriend was there." In the end, the chief relinquished, "I've ordered the case closed. There's not much we can do."

Left among the survivors, Coffey reflects, "Nobody wants to think about their own mortality. You don't think about it until it happens to you."

chapter thirteen
Leelanau Peninsula

The quiet fishing Village of Leland was stirred from its winter sleep when Dr. Kevorkian paid a call to Stanley L. Ball's house facing North Lake Leelanau. Ball's woeful old beagle, Flash, sprawled on the front porch.

Though Kevorkian does not like to travel, he drove north to make his first official call outside of Oakland and Macomb Counties. This 500 person Village of Leland is nestled about 300 miles northwest of Detroit on Lake Michigan -- called *The Third Coast* -- at the tip of Michigan's "little finger," in the mitten of the lower peninsula. Early Native Americans from the Ottawa and Chippewa tribes had called the peninsula "Leelanau" meaning "the delight of life" or "land of delight."

Ball was not complicated; what you see is what you get: he was a muscular man, active in the local 4-H Club who took club members skiing, both cross-country and downhill. He once tried out for the 1932 U.S. Olympic Team in Greco-Roman wrestling but didn't place.

He often walked the mile each way into town and back to eat breakfast with the "townies" at the Early Bird Inn on Main Street in Leland. Ball was a real flirt, very much a ladies man after his wife died. "He used to walk down here to eat every day. He'd always give me a hug," recounted waitress Dora Grant.

Northport photographer David Brigham recalls Ball's warmth and wit. "I can see Stanley walking up to the Bluebird Restaurant now. On New Year's Eve and St. Patrick's Day, Stanley would walk in to the Bluebird carrying his clarinet. Whenever Stanley walked through the door -- had there been a fireplace -- we would have thrown another log on the fire. Stanley would sit right over there," pointed Brigham, "charming us with his jokes and witty sayings, swapping lies, playing his clarinet and harmonica until all that was left were the embers of a night of good cheer."

"He could tell great stories, had a great sense of humor," recollected Ed Kahrs, 85, a retired farmer who knew Ball as the Agricultural Director of Leelanau County Cooperative Extension Service from 1945-1969.

Before World War II Ball personally, but privately, objected when his employer, the U.S. Department of Agriculture, directed agriculture agents to "talk up war to the farmers because it's inevitable." Opposed to such pressure tactics, one day Ball quietly hung a sign on his office door that read *Gone Fishin' -- Bye!* He never returned.

In his life, farmer Ball had planted over 100,000 trees in Leelanau County. But the past few years had been unkind to him. Though his modest bungalow sat on the sparkling west shore of North Lake Leelanau, where Ball lived since 1948, he no longer could enjoy the view. Cancer had stolen his sight.

Given his failing vision over the past two years, in order to collect his mail, Ball had to grope his way

174

along a length of cord stretching from his front door, down the porch steps and out to the mail box. He would use this same technique in front of his home where he would exercise for a half hour each day.

Ball's wife, Elizabeth, had died some years earlier. Nonetheless, Ball had been active until one month before his medicide when he was diagnosed with inoperable pancreatic cancer, one of the most painful forms which smothered his light-hearted charm and joviality. Ball put no stock in the afterlife; to him you were just gone.

Ball was exhausted but, with humor, he would say "This is the life of a pig. I eat. And I go to the bathroom. I sleep. I itch. I scratch. Around and around and around.

Ball never waivered in his resolve saying, "I am not afraid of dying or of being dead. I am afraid of the terrible, uncontrollable pain and of the loss of control."

There was also Mary Biernat's agony.

MARY BIERNAT'S SECRET

Breast cancer had attacked Biernat 15 years ago and she had undergone a mastectomy. She had been in and out of the hospital for two years. No doubt, Biernat had been sick for a long time before her husband, Frank, died of cancer in 1988. Recently, her own cancer had resurfaced in her spine and lungs. Biernat hid her resurgent cancer as long as she could.

On Monday, February 3, 1992, Julie Bryja, Biernat's sister-in-law from Merrilville, Indiana, spent two hours at Biernat's home in Crown Pointe, Indiana, 50 miles southeast of Chicago. Biernat was in good spirits. They talked about old times, like when they would go to church festivals and shopping. There were so many good memories. Biernat had always been fun to be with, until her illness took its toll

175

"Hang in there," Bryja urged when leaving that Monday. "I will pray for you."

"Don't pray for me," Biernat chided. "I can't live with the pain. It's impossible."

Biernat was a good Catholic. She never discussed her looming suicide with her sister-in-law. But as often as they were together, Biernat had never mentioned Kevorkian's name.

On Tuesday, stepdaughter Linda Penn, of Schereville, Indiana, telephoned the ailing Biernat who was in ghastly pain. "I am very sick," Biernat reported. "And I really don't want any visitors." Still, there was no mention of suicide. Penn sent flowers.

On Wednesday, the frail, 80 pound Biernat traveled by car north from Lakes of the Four Seasons, 15 miles southeast of Gary, Indiana. Biernat was driven to Leland in a rented van by her son, Dennis V. Vajner and another son, Ronald.

On Thursday, with her two sons by her side as well as Camilla Conlon, her 26 year old granddaughter, Biernat arrived at the last stop of her last journey.

THE FINAL JOURNEY

Biernat, 73, joined Ball, then 82, in his home on Michigan's Leelanau Peninsula. Indiana had a law prohibiting coerced suicides, but not assisted suicides. Not wanting to risk prosecution in another state, Kevorkian refused to journey south to Indiana. This would be Kevorkian's third double-suicide.

The obitiatrist had been counseling these two cancer patients for more than a month, both over the telephone and through letters. Ball and Biernat had not become acquainted with each other until the day before they died. As a group, the evening before, they all shared a wonderful last supper, ordering take-out Chinese. Ball ate Peking Duck and drank red wine.

Each pulled small metal rings connected to plastic tubes and metal containers. The lethal carbon monoxide/nitrogen mixture was released into the face masks each had strapped on, stealing their breath of life. Both inhaled the poison gases from Kevorkian-supplied canisters, similar to the squat propane tanks that feed gas barbecues used in the many vacation homes found in that resort area. The secret plans for their medicides would soon cease to be a private matter.

SUMMONING THE SHERIFF

On Thursday, February 4, about 12:35 p.m., S. David Ball, 45, telephoned the Leelanau County sheriff to report, "This is David Ball and my father has committed suicide." Ball's body was on the living room couch and Biernat's body was on another couch in the sun room to the south. Kevorkian had come to The County.

"When I got the call, I thought maybe it was a joke," said Leelanau County Prosecutor G. Thomas Aylsworth. "I can't believe that something like this would happen here." Aylsworth rushed to the scene, flailing about, posturing, threatening, judging. Aylsworth wanted to haul Kevorkian to jail, but Kevorkian had beaten the deadline, performing these medicides before the suicide ban had taken affect. Despite a shouting match on the back porch, Aylsworth never had Kevorkian arrested.

But Detective Sergeant Robert W. Mead was unruffled as he briefed reporters and photographers outside Ball's home. "It appears to be the same old deal," he said casually.

Janus and Nicol were in attendance. Kevorkian was taken into custody and strided silently to the police car which whisked him away from Ball's house.

Prosecutor Aylsworth characterized Kevorkian, the man, as "a nice guy" and remarked: "The thing that really struck me is how business-like it all was," even though Kevorkian accepted no fees from the families involved.

Indeed, after less than an hour of questioning, Prosecutor Aylsworth released Kevorkian shortly before 3:30 p.m. Then Aylsworth announced to the press: "It's my understanding that Dr. Kevorkian is on his way back to Southfield -- where I hope he stays."

Deviating from the path taken by the Oakland County Coroner, Dr. Matthew A. Houghton, Jr., the Leelanau County Medical Examiner, instead, ruled these deaths were suicides, not homicides.

RELATIVE REACTIONS

One of the 1,642 year-round residents of this picturesque resort community grumbled, "That's all we needed for Kevorkian to come up here. Next thing you know, we'll have 5,000 people coming up here wanting to look around," moaned Roy Buckler, 86, a native of the Leelanau Peninsula.

Stanley Biernat, Mary Biernat's brother-in-law, at first was surprised to hear the news, then saddened. What about suicide? "I never had a thought like that myself," Stanley Biernat reflected. "I don't know if people who commit suicide are weak or if it's the pain."

Late Thursday afternoon along North Lake Leelanau, Reverend Paul Zimmerman, age 75, Traverse City, Michigan, was performing corporal works of mercy -- making house calls ministering to the sick. Only when he visited the Ball's bungalow did the Reverend first learn about the double suicide earlier in the day when Ball made his final exit.

"It is God who gives life and it is God who takes it away," the parson preached. But just as quickly as he had invoked God, the Reverend Zimmerman began worrying about himself, lamenting that, "Pretty soon, some might think old people are a nuisance."

State Senator George McManus, R-Traverse City, had talked with his long-time friend, Ball, only two or three days before his death. "Stanley told me he had pancreatic cancer and was getting ready to exit," McManus confessed. "But he didn't talk about medicide." But McManus should not have been surprised by Ball's secretiveness because he knew that McManus was opposed to assisted suicide.

Looking out at the sun sparkling on the ice of Sutton's Bay, long-time acquaintance Joyce Bahle, reflected on Ball's delight of life: "It's a gorgeous day out here and I say, *God bless Stanley Ball.* He lived a classy life and I'm proud of him."

Bahle felt that "Stanley was giving a message. He was a pioneer in an age group and as a male, willing to stand out and say, '*I'm not afraid of death. I believe in medicide.*'

"Maybe Stanley is saying to the future generation, '*There will be a world of choice.*'"

GONE FISHIN'

For Ball, there would be no funeral or memorial service; he would not subject his family to such maudlin indignities. "Maybe a champagne toast," Ball allowed, "and toss my ashes in Lake Leelanau."

An obituary of Ball was handwritten by his daughter, Judy Sorum Brown, 48, Hyattsville, Maryland. Though Ball died on February 4, Brown had transcribed her father's obituary dated January 27. The exact date of her father's suicide was scheduled ten days before.

". . . I feared if I stayed [in Michigan], I would be unwilling to relinquish Dad to that journey which he planned for himself," Brown revealed. When she spoke with her father the night before his medicide, Ball reported, "The journey is on and I can't wait."

DR. DEATH

Brown was not with her father when he died. While she knew of his planned medicide and was supportive, she didn't know exactly when it would occur.

Ironically, when her father died about 12:35 p.m., Brown had been conducting a seminar entitled "Freedom of the Human Spirit." She was an independent educator and consultant.

Not aware of the hour of her father's death and out of reach by phone, Brown had left her seminar and was driving her car across the long ribbon of the Bay Bridge which spanned Chesapeake Bay. While the sun sparkled on the Bay, Ball's name led the 2:00 p.m. National Public Radio news. "I was stunned," Brown said.

She explained that her father's death was merely an extension of his quiet, self-assured, individual style. "The manner of his death is absolutely consistent with the rest of his life," she shared.

"It's just like the sign Dad hung from his office door years ago -- *Gone Fishin' -- Bye!*."

chapter fourteen

Then
There Were Twelve

With two medicides earlier that week up north in Michigan's Leelanau Peninsula, Elaine Goldbaum would become the third person in several days to end her life with Kevorkian, the agent of death, in attendance.

A severe victim of multiple sclerosis, Goldbaum, was to become the twelfth patient since June 1990 aided in suicide by Kevorkian.

Indeed, in the past two months, as many people had ended their lives with his assistance as had done so in the previous 30 months.

Many of Kevorkian's patients were nervous about the April 1 impending suicide ban in Michigan. While not rushing patients into hasty decisions because of any deadline, nonetheless Dr. Kevorkian was quickening his pace: deaths were arranged to beat the looming criminalization of medicide. According to one *Detroit Free Press* editor, Kevorkian is "cramming as many suicides into his schedule as possible. Who said incentives don't matter?"

NO CHANCE OF RECOVERY

At the young age of 47, Goldbaum was legally blind and, since 1988, had been confined to a wheelchair by her muscular disease. Less than two months earlier, her treating physician, Dr. William Leuchter, said Goldbaum had "no chance of recovery."

One week after that grim assessment by her physician, Goldbaum petitioned Kevorkian for help writing:

Dear Dr. Kevorkian:

I cannot do anything for myself. ...I can no longer continue living like this. The quality of my life is totally diminished.

I am Jewish and have been raised to believe that suicide is a mortal sin. Dr. Jack Kevorkian, your assistance in medicide will get me into heaven.

Elaine Goldbaum

Pondering this Judeo-Christian ethic which makes suicide a moral sin, Goldbaum may have reflected upon the words of Roman Catholic Archbishop Adam Maida, Archdiocese of Detroit:

In a strange sort of way, as the saying goes, suffering is good for the soul because it draws us out of ourselves and helps us be more sensitive to others and our need for them. When we come face to face with people who are suffering, we learn to see the real value of a person -- the gift of life itself.

182

But to Goldbaum, such spiritual nostrums could not change her mind. The martyrs of Masada, the crucifixion of Christ, the hemlock eaten by Socrates all taught us that we sometimes respect life by etching out our own death — which is not always the enemy.

A bad death was to be avoided as much as a bad life. There are no good shortcuts to avoiding pain in life. Mere existence is sometimes worth the price, though sometimes not. Goldbaum's existence had become a pageant of hopeless suffering pursuing the vain desire of a decent death. She wanted to embrace a death that was better than her life of overwhelming pain. Goldbaum craved a good death. She was seeking to restore a sense of peace and order.

If the Archbishop were to visit her, would he ask that she persevere solely for the sake of suffering? Would this Holy Man be the judge of how much suffering is too much for Goldbaum? Despair was the only fruit of her suffering. If she endured, would that make her a sacrificial lamb, guaranteed an ascent into heaven?

Lost in her thoughts, Goldbaum wondered, "Would the Archbishop -- who believes eternity in heaven is guaranteed by the amount of suffering on Earth -- be surprised when God judges him for the compassion he has shown to the suffering by not urging them to prolong their pain?" Goldbaum didn't seem to understand; in the Archbishop's mind, did a "good Christian" believe in long sentences for criminals, long suffering for the elderly and prolonged death for the infirm?

Goldbaum decided that suffering for its own sake was not so rewarding as the Archbishop made it out to be. If suffering were good for the soul, then she had evolved into goodness itself. She valued the concept of a good death. To the Archbishop, that may have been a curious concept, but Goldbaum now chose to dance with death.

Kevorkian has been confronted with the role religion plays in his medicide procedure: "I've had all kinds of religions," Kevorkian said, "and not one wanted a religious consultation. Religion is totally irrelevant to what they want." While of Armenian descent, Kevorkian's own religious views are unknown; he appears philosophically driven by the type of humanism and caring expected of a practitioner of the healing arts.

On Monday morning, February 8, 1993, at the Franklin Pointe Apartments in Southfield, Michigan, Goldbaum donned the same style mask as so many others had worn. She tugged on a little string which released a clip, allowing a fatal flow of carbon monoxide into the mask, ending her life. She died about 10:30 a.m., in plenty of time for her medicide to make the evening news.

IT'S NOT EASY

Kevorkian says it's not easy watching someone die, but it's something physicians must do all the time. Kevorkian has confided that tears came to his eyes several times while he was the attending physician at medicides.

"It's tough on me. You've got to steel yourself. Every doctor does. If a doctor didn't do that, he couldn't function. Medicine is a real tragic profession in most cases. You steel yourself and you cannot empathize too much, although I do."

Dr. Kevorkian has described the mood in an assisted suicide:

Well, it's not pleasant, of course and one would know that. And it's hard to put into words. It's a great mixture of things. But it's not pleasant, not at all.

Some are very moving though. In several cases, I've wept a little and tears have come down my cheeks and I've felt embarrassed and I said, "Wait a minute. You're a doctor. What are you crying for?"

You can't help it in some cases when a person's dying, with loved ones there, with music they love playing in the room and a friend reading the Twenty-Third Psalm to them. That seems too moving and it moved me.

It's a great mixture, and every incident is different. You can't characterize it one way.

Kevorkian has recounted that "These are not happy moments. The ending of a human life can never be a good moment." He considers the loss of a human life negative under all circumstances.

INVESTIGATIVE DEMANDS

Oakland County Prosecutor Richard Thompson has been impotent to stop Kevorkian thus far because court after court tosses out the murder charges which Thompson has levied against the obitiatrist.

But the Michigan legislature was in the process of drafting bills to provide prosecutors with more tools to investigate crime. The proposed legislation would award county prosecutors sweeping powers to wiretap telephones, obtain no-knock search warrants and issue "investigative demands" to reluctant witnesses.

Thompson had told legislators he needed these powers for investigations into assisted suicides because family and friends in attendance join a conspiracy of silence. "So often in these kinds of cases," Thompson admonished, "there are witnesses who refuse to talk to police, or they lie to police. The public has to realize that the law [forbidding lies to police] will not be effective without this bill."

Aghast, Fieger has lashed out at Thompson as "a sick mother____er and you can quote me." But in a more relaxed moment, Fieger would reflect on Thompson musing, "He's a real cold fish. A nice little swastika would warm up his office considerably."

AN IMMEDIATE BAN

With the death of Goldbaum, the Michigan legislature -- having already passed legislation outlawing assisted suicide -- debated whether to make their ban *immediate*. It promised to be one law written to prohibit one man from doing one thing.

"You have to realize," one observer cautioned, "the people who Dr. Kevorkian helped came to him -- he did not go to them."

Fieger said that an *immediate* ban would indicate that Michigan's lawmakers are manipulated by "a right-wing fanatic religious minority" led by Right to Life.

ON TO OHIO

While Kevorkian has been contacted by hundreds of people interested in suicide, far more of his patients go on to die natural deaths than the few who have died through medicide.

No doubt, Kevorkian turns away many patients, as he recounts, "People call up and say, '*I'm diabetic*,' '*I've got heart disease*.' You know they can go on. That's not terminal, that's not critical. Many psychiatric cases . . . and you know they are in agony. Some people have told me from the age of 4 to 35, they've never wanted to live. These cases don't qualify. I don't even consider them."

However, in passing, Kevorkian did mention that he was counseling three people in Ohio, without identifying them or their diseases. When asked if he would travel to Ohio, Kevorkian refused to say for sure, leaving his foot in the door.

With the hint that Kevorkian might like to ply his lethal trade in Ohio, one editor of *The Detroit News* noted that "A bus ticket from Detroit to Toledo costs $11. We will pay Kevorkian's fare -- one-way."

Though Kevorkian doesn't discuss particular patients or medicide plans in advance, Fieger teased, "Jack has potential clients in Ohio. He's itching to get across the state line -- he's itching. I hope he doesn't go because they have the death penalty, the electric chair in Ohio."

Ohio lawmakers were inflamed at the prospect of Kevorkian's threatened arrival. Legislators reacted swiftly to the news by yanking away the welcome mat and introducing legislation to ban assisted suicide.

Fieger charged that opposition to medicide in the Buckeye State was being led by "radical right-wing groups that want to take the right of choice away from the people."

But anti-Kevorkian forces were not dissuaded. "We hope the [Ohio] legislature will take immediate action on it. With [Kevorkian] extending his tentacles, so to speak, in Ohio, we're leery and fearful that this will happen and we want to get on top of it right away," professed the Catholic Conference of Ohio.

With Ohio doing everything in its collective power to stop him, the acid-tongued Kevorkian taunted back saying, "Had I known it was [legal in Ohio until now], I would have gone farther with a couple of patients there in the past."

DR. DEATH

Kevorkian promised that Ohio patients who need his services can travel to Michigan. "It's almost as effective if they come here and get it done. Patients will have to come here. Those who can't travel will have to keep suffering because of the barbaric authorities . . . down there in Ohio."

Kevorkian was unrestrained as the defiant, self-righteous and ridiculing critic of his opponents. He unleashed a verbal assault against Governor George Voinovich and Ohio State Senator Grace Drake, R-Solon:

> *The Governor was born three centuries too late. He would love to light a torch to burn people at the stake. He'd love to do it. And That Woman would love to light the torch at the stake too.*

> *These people are inquisitional. Their minds are crazed with a divine mission. They want to perpetuate suffering.*

> *. . . .Ohio legislators are very much like Michigan's. They are controlled by the religious right. It shows that we are still in the dark ages.*

Fieger has seethed at government interference with the individual right to die, fuming that it is ". . . reprehensible that these religious fanatics think they are doing God's work by seeking to deny citizens the right to decide their own destinies. . . ."

Fieger also condemned the religious right for the widespread turmoil over medicide. "We really don't care whether they . . . like it or not. They're not going to impose their religion on the backs of the people . . .

[which will only] increase individual suffering. I think those people are dangerous to society."

Yet in the end, Kevorkian conceded that he would not go to Ohio because the prosecutors "are like sharks waiting for me. They want to put me in prison even though there's no law" banning medicide.

Kevorkian, now age 64, questioned, "Who would step into that kind of anarchy? Nazi Germany was milder than that."

chapter fifteen

Take Off the Mask

Hugh Gale once was robust. A sailor in the U.S. merchant marines for 15 years, he had last toiled as a security guard. Now age 70, Gale was sickly and afflicted by chronic emphysema and congestive heart disease. He had been miserable for years. Often, he would pray that he would not wake up in the morning.

Gale had contemplated suicide by a drug overdose. He also thought about using a gun, but that was too messy and he didn't know where to get such a weapon at any rate.

Some say Gale was panic stricken by the Michigan legislature's ban on assisted suicide that threatened to limit his options. Above all, however, Gale wanted to be able to control his own death.

Just before Christmas 1992, his wife Cheryl remarked, "I don't know what to get you for Christmas because you don't go out and you don't need clothes. What would you like for Christmas?"

Gale matter-of-factly replied, "I would like an appointment with Dr. Kevorkian."

Cheryl Gale hesistantly laughed and countered, "No, really, what would you like for Christmas?"

Gale steadfastly repeated, "I would like an appointment with Dr. Kevorkian."

SPECIAL DEATH COUNSELING

Gale got his Christmas wish at last. Once he consulted with Kevorkian, who promised to help, a tremendous peace came over him. He was a different person. Gale had made his decision: he was going to do what he wanted to do. For the next several months, the obitiatrist counseled with the former marine.

When Kevorkian made a house call four nights before Gale died, neighbor Cheryl Kennedy was peering out of her window and declared, "I saw Jack Kevorkian leave the house . . . and I told everybody and they thought I was nuts."

Kennedy also allowed, "I knew [Hugh Gale] was sick and I knew he's never been out of the house." Indeed, Gale had not left his home for the past three years.

That previous Thursday night before he died, Gale expressed concern to Kevorkian about how the lethal carbon monoxide might affect him, given his emphysema. Gale wanted his exit to be easy. "I don't want to be going out hard," Gale admonished the doctor.

When Kevorkian told Gale he would have to wait until the following week for the medicide procedure, Gale protested asking, "Can't we make tonight the final session? Because I want to end my life. . . .Make it as soon as possible."

Though Kevorkian urged Gale to enjoy at least one thing every day, Gale persisted, "There's not much joy in living for me."

30,000 SUICIDES EACH YEAR

Less than one week later, on Monday, February 15, 1993, Kevorkian attended his first medicide in Macomb County, Michigan. Gale was the second male to take his own life in Kevorkian's presence.

Gale's death was the thirteenth Kevorkian medicide, a minuscule number compared to the 30,000 U.S. suicides annually. But you would have thought he was responsible for every one given some of the public outcry.

Before determining to make his final exit, Gale had been disabled for more than a decade. He lived strapped to a can of oxygen, with breathing tubes protruding from his nostrils, often turning blue and constantly gasping for breath.

Gale had 18 percent breathing capacity. He was unable to walk to the bathroom and back. He literally suffocated daily as his lungs would lock up. His constant fear of suffocation was real. He frequently lost consciousness and would black out. It was a daily death.

Though the Roseville Police arrived quickly after the report of Gale's suicide, by the time they had surrounded his house with yellow crime scene tape, Gale had long since abandoned his ghastly pain.

When the police entered the tiny white house where the Gales had lived seventeen years, Gale's body was slumping in the living room chair where he last reclined. At Gale's side was a canister filled with carbon monoxide. He had placed a mask over his face, sucking in the deadly gas from a tank supplied by Kevorkian.

Gale gasped his last breath at 9:55 a.m., in plenty of time to make that day's prime time news.

With search warrant in hand and wearing rubber gloves, Roseville police arrived, picking through Gale's home, collecting evidence and shooting videotape. All the while, Gale's body sat upright in a chair, half-covered with an afghan. His face was covered with a gas mask and his left finger tied to a string which unleashed poison gases from the nearby tank of carbon monoxide.

While Gale had five sons, ages 34 to 52, living out of state, Cheryl, his wife of 22 years, was the only relative present when he died. Cheryl had witnessed her husband begging for the end. Her deeper love and compassion let him go, rather than selfishly keeping her husband alive until the very end of what had by then become his miserable life. "The real tragedy is not what Kevorkian may have done," admonished Cheryl Gale, "but the patients who are suffering their last days on Earth. Medical technology and drugs have kept people alive long past their time for a graceful passing, dooming them to extreme agony."

Neighbor Dona Park reflected about the Gales saying "They kept to themselves." Hugh and Cheryl Gale were so private in their intentions that one of Gale's in-law's surprisingly first heard news of his death on television.

PROSECUTORIAL PROMISES

Macomb County Prosecutor Carl Marlinga put everyone on alert saying, "I think Kevorkian is on a crusade and a lot more people will die."

Kevorkian's attorney Schwartz predicted that Marlinga would be a "prize fool" if he prosecuted Kevorkian for Gale's death.

Neither of Kevorkian's attorneys are paid a penny for representing their infamous client. They are adequately compensated, however, by the public relations gained plus whatever psychic income they might earn.

"I will not obey that law because that law is immoral," Kevorkian warned. "I will continue to assist humans to alleviate their agony and interminable suffering. Yes and if that means they have to kill themselves to do it, then yes."

Take Off the Mask

Kevorkian conceded that he may be arrested for his practice of medicide: "To go to jail is the ultimate slavery. If I have lost my freedom, I have lost something more valuable than life. Therefore, continuing life becomes pointless. It's as simple as that."

If jailed, Kevorkian promised he would stage a hunger strike. "I will stop eating. Whenever I am in jail, my liberty has been taken away unjustly. Therefore, I will stop eating. In effect, the state will assist my suicide." Admitting that he might die before trial, Kevorkian proclaimed:

I am willing to die. . . . not to be a martyr, not for protest, not for pity. I don't do it for that reason. Only for one reason. The reason Thoreau did it: because my liberty is unjustly taken away.

People might say I'm a zealot. I just stick to my principles. Was Patrick Henry a zealot? Was Thoreau a zealot? Was Margaret Sanger a zealot? Was Mandella a zealot? I follow their example.

At first, Marlinga promised he would not press charges if he was satisfied that Gale committed suicide. He even pledged not to arrest Kevorkian unless the doctor had actually been the one to activate the lever which released the carbon monoxide into Gale's mask. At least that's what the prosecutor promised initially.

"I find it distasteful the arrogant way in which Kevorkian self-righteously feels he is the only one who knows the truth on this issue," griped Marlinga. But the smell of politics wafted through the air: not many weeks earlier, Marlinga had declared his candidacy for U.S. Senate in the next year's election.

PICKING THROUGH GARBAGE

After Gale's death and without a word, Kevorkian exited the Gale's nondescript ranch home, unexceptional in this blue collar neighborhood, slightly north of the Motor City. Likewise, assistants Janus and Nicol left without comment.

In the past, Fieger had branded Kevorkian's opponents as "Nazis" and "religious nuts." That was heard as a "Call to Arms" by Operation Rescue, a pro-life group that had made its reputation rummaging through trash receptacles at abortion clinics. Activists from around the country swarmed into metropolitan Detroit to condemn his renegade method of mercy killing.

"We are going to meddle," pledged Dawn Stover of Advocates for Life Ministries, based in Portland, Oregon. "We have got to stop Jack Kevorkian." Right to Life advocates wanted to assure that "Jack Kevorkian does not kill again."

Making good on the promise to interfere, Lynn Mills, a Right to Life activist, targeted Kevorkian's long-time associate, Nicol. She staked out Nicol's Waterford Township house, the site of three previous medicides. When Nicol tossed out two garbage bags for curbside pickup, the anti-abortion activist confiscated his rubbish.

Mills confessed that she drove down Nicol's residential street and stopped at his curb. Leaping from her vehicle, Mills simply tossed the two white, kitchen-sized bags of Nicol's trash with yellow twist ties into her car and drove back to her own home. "I was in the right place at the right time," Mills boasted. "It was unbelievable, providential."

Trash left at the curb is legally considered abandoned property and anybody can take it. As a private citizen, Mills worked for no police agency and needed no warrant to seize Nicol's leftovers. "On two separate grounds, it's perfectly admissible in court," Marlinga later rationalized. "It's unsavory and I don't like it," he apologized, "but it's admissible."

Prepped and ready at Mills' home were three other anti-abortion activists. Slipping on surgical gloves and respiratory masks, the quartet dumped Nicol's garbage on a tiled floor at Mills' home. Sifting through the debris, they found a crumpled, stained Final Action form: it was a one-page, preliminary report of Gale's medicide procedure. The Final Action form was typewritten and carried the signature of Kevorkian.

The expropriated document read like a set of minutes, chronicling one version about Gale's medicide. The quartet pushed back their tears as they studied each syllable of every last word.

The Final Action form, at first, disclosed that, about 45 seconds after Gale put on the face mask, he became "flushed and agitated, breathing deeply saying '*Take it off!*'" Then he calmed down.

SUPPLEMENTING THE REPORT

Cheryl Gale said -- where the Final Action form was silent -- that her husband panicked, gasping, "Take it off. Take it off," meaning the oxygen tent in which he was sitting. Kevorkian had devised an oxygen tent for Gale to recirculate the carbon monoxide and hasten Gale's death.

Kevorkian also contended that they removed a tent surrounding Gale which had prevented the carbon monoxide from escaping into the living room. "I know it was very uncomfortable for you. Let's just stop," Kevorkian had advised his patient, "I can come back another day if you still want this."

Kevorkian insisted, ". . .I wanted to stop. I told him, '*Let's do this another day.*'"

But Gale pleaded to Kevorkian, "Please don't make me wait any longer; let's get on with it."

DR. DEATH

Gale persisted and never abandoned his determination to die. Cheryl Gale and Kevorkian sat with Gale about 15-20 minutes. "The patient wanted to continue," said Kevorkian.

Finally, Gale fixed a determined look upon Kevorkian, demanding "Let's get on with it."

THE REPORT CONTINUES

The silent Operation Rescue quartet, still fighting the tears, continued poring over the purloined Final Action report:

> *After about 20 minutes, with nasal oxygen continuing, the mask was replaced over his nose and mouth and [Hugh Gale] again pulled the clip off the crimped tubing [which allowed the carbon monoxide to flow into the face mask].*

The discarded version of the Final Action report then continued to read:

> *In 30-35 seconds, [Gale] again flushed, became agitated with moderate hyperpnea,* and immediately after saying 'Take it off' once again, he fell into unconsciousness. The mask was then left in place. Hyperpnea continued for 35-40 seconds, after which a slower and calmer breathing pattern ensued, lasting about eight minutes, gradually diminishing in rate and intensity. Heartbeat was undetectable about three minutes after last breath.*

After about 12 minutes in total, Gale's heart stopped

---

* *Hyperpnea* means abnormally rapid or deep breathing.

beating. This Final Action form apparently was signed by Kevorkian and supposedly witnessed by Cheryl Gale, Janus and Nicol.

NIGHT MOVES

Prosecutor Marlinga immediately pronounced that the Final Action form retrieved by Mills "suggests that the death was involuntary and that at the last minute the patient changed his mind."

Marlinga directed his investigators to converge on Kevorkian's Main Street apartment in Royal Oak and on Nicol's home in Waterford Township. In their raids, the constabulary seized the original Final Action form maintained by Kevorkian for his patient records.

Fieger sneered that Marlinga's raid on Kevorkian's apartment smacked of "fascism in the middle of the night."

HUGH GALE WAS "AIR HUNGRY"

Even after reading Operation Rescue's poached document, medical experts did not believe Gale was having second thoughts. When the carbon monoxide initially flooded the face mask, Gale asked that the tent be removed. His agitation, rapid breathing and apparent panic were not signs that Gale was rescinding his suicide request. Instead, these were indications of oxygen depletion.

One anesthesiologist noted that Gale "must have felt uncomfortable because he was air-hungry." Dr. Samir Fuleihan of Harper Hospital, Detroit, explained, "You are awake and your oxygen's getting borderline. You're going to try to struggle to breathe."

Though Jack Kevorkian, M.D. was a pathologist by training, his medical career had focused on performing autopsies. Despite his medical training, he may not have anticipated that Gale would gasp for breath before succumbing. In his last moments, Gale would be breathing air with less than 10 percent oxygen.

When oxygen-dependent patients are deprived of air, they get disoriented, agitated, begin to hyperventilate, and get confused and combative. Gale reacted with panic, like a drowning man going under for the third time, unable to breathe. These are symptoms of oxygen depletion, not that Gale was changing his mind.

Since Kevorkian's medical license had been suspended in Michigan, he had no choice but to use carbon monoxide with Gale, despite his chronic emphysema. The Mercitron was no longer an option because prescription drugs were required for its operation.

The Mercitron involves no breathing, it is intervenous and relies upon thiopental, a fast-acting barbiturate that produces almost instantaneous unconsciousness after a single dose and potassium chloride which paralyzes the heart muscle. Without a medical license, the potassium chloride and pentothal, available by prescription, were unavailable to the obitiatrist. Much faster than his carbon monoxide/nitrogen mixture, the Mercitron offers a merciful death by injection in minutes.

MURDER, NOT MERCY KILLING

For three years, Kevorkian had eluded authorities as he practiced his gruesome campaign. So Marlinga was swift to rattle his prosecutorial sabre, intimating that he was weighing murder charges against Kevorkian in the death of Gale.

"There's no doubt that if the evidence is authenticated," Marlinga expounded, "we would be moving out of the area of assisted suicide and could be looking toward possible homicide charges."

Others were less restrained. "It's murder, not mercy killing," advocated Dawn Stover, suggesting a cover up.

"Dr. Kevorkian portrays himself as an Angel of Mercy. He's not. Mr. Gale makes that clear."

Fieger castigated these foes as "A bunch of right-wing Christian nuts [who] again called Kevorkian a murderer. It's laughable."

One self-described Christian was supposedly offended by Fieger's comment and complained to Michigan's Attorney Grievance Commission. An investigation of attorney Fieger was launched because his comment about Christians allegedly constituted attorney misconduct. Fieger countered that the investigation was improper and urged the Michigan Supreme Court to intervene.

Not to be outdone, Operation Rescue's Reverend Patrick Mahoney elevated the chorus to a din and bleated that "Hugh Gale did not die with dignity. He died an agonizing death. He pleaded that the mask be taken off. This was clearly a murder taking place. Mr. Gale did not want to die."

Adding fuel to the fire, Reverend Mahoney accused Fieger of taking "the legal profession down the same path as Mr. Kevorkian has [taken] the medical profession -- to the pits of hell. [Fieger's] not even an ambulance chaser, he's a hearse chaser. He's a disgrace to the [legal] profession."

When Dawn Stover approached Fieger near his office ostensibly to speak with him, she indicted the barrister accusingly saying, "He charged at my vehicle with a baseball bat, running, screaming, cussing and yelling."

Asked if he attacked, Fieger rancorously acknowledged, "Absolutely I did. If they come back, I'll take the biggest bat I can find to them. I'm not going to be intimidated by these religious loonies. It's a joke."

THE CRITICAL DIFFERENCE

Police officials tried to argue that Kevorkian's discarded version of the Final Action report indicated that

201

Gale asked -- on two different occasions -- that the mask be removed. But, both copies of the Final Action report agree Gale's mask was removed after the first request.

The trashed edition of the statement, however, indicates that Gale made a second request to "Take it off" and nothing was done. Differently, Kevorkian's "final draft" had deleted any reference to Gale's second plea to "Take it off."

The critical difference between Kevorkian's official Final Action report, and the filthy form fished from Nicol's pilfered garbage bag, was this: in Nicol's discarded version, Gale supposedly **twice** asked Kevorkian to remove the mask but, allegedly, Kevorkian did nothing on the **second request**, permitting Gale to die.

Differently on Kevorkian's version of the Final Action form, he allegedly was trying to fix a mistake, not cover up anything. Kevorkian's copy had the second reference to "Take it off" whited out and changed. Correction fluid was used to opaque out 38 words, changing the description of the death and deleting the second reference to Gale's request . . . to "Take it off," meaning the oxygen tent in which Gale was sitting.

That scrapped document was supposedly a rough draft. Kevorkian allegedly corrected that "rough draft" after showing it to Nicol and Janus who said, "Wait a second, you got a mistake here." And Kevorkian said, "Yeah, there's a mistake here," and he rectified the original which he kept; the mistaken version was tossed in the garbage at Nicol's house.

The two different versions of the Final Action report raised public speculation about whether Kevorkian had gone too far: Had Gale changed his mind about dying? If so, did Dr. Death turn a deaf ear to the second plea by Gale to "Take it off"? Should Kevorkian have intervened to abort Gale's efforts to kill himself?

Fieger charged that the Final Action form pilfered by

Mills from Nicol's rubbish was altered. Fieger explained the differing versions of the report:

> *After each suicide, Dr. Kevorkian makes one of the standard [Final Action] reports out. While making this report out, nearly two weeks after the suicide occurred, [Dr. Kevorkian] realized he had repeated a line [by inadvertently stating that Gale had made a second demand to remove the mask] and discarded it. The one they found in the trash isn't correct.*

PERMITTING SUICIDE IS NO CRIME

Alleging that he just wanted to sort things out, Prosecutor Marlinga said he was looking into convening a coroner's inquest which, like a grand jury, can compel testimony. Unlike a grand jury, however, a coroner's inquest is not secret. Marlinga was prepared to offer immunity from prosecution to bystanders who would testify against Kevorkian.

However, no crime could have been committed even if Kevorkian refused a second plea by Gale to "Take off the mask" -- which Kevorkian disputes. James Thorburn, retired chief judge of the Oakland County Circuit Court observed: "If I see you slicing up somebody with an ax and I do nothing, I'm not guilty of a crime."

"There is no criminal penalty for not stopping someone in the middle of their suicide," correctly explained Kevorkian's attorney Schwartz.

WORRIED ABOUT STALKERS

As this hullabaloo was stirring, Kevorkian began noticing that he was being stalked. Cars with two and three occupants would park outside of his Main Street apartment in downtown Royal Oak, Michigan monitoring his movements. Some mornings, the stalkers were parked both at his front and back doors. It's not that Kevorkian was paranoid, but everywhere he looked, they were there.

Kevorkian complained to the Royal Oak police. "We had a call of a suspicious person outside the apartment building and a report was taken," acknowledged Sergeant Doug Wolfe. Only when Kevorkian threatened to criminally prosecute these activists under Michigan's recently enacted anti-stalking law did their surveillance stop.

Lobbyists from The Catholic Campaign of America soon sounded the alarm, warning of apathy and unenthusiastic local opposition to Dr. Death. A national collection of prominent Catholics who oppose euthanasia rallied to raise funds to fight Kevorkian's efforts.

But Fieger exhorted, "We need more of these people around us like we need a hole in our heads. These people are religious terrorists."

In quick reply, a grass-roots group called "The Friends of Dr. Kevorkian" materialized. Founder Dawn Haselhuhn, Ortonville, Michigan, complained, "People in the Right-to-Life movement have pressured the legislature and governor to take away our right to choose." Haselhuhn's *Friends* promised to "show the state legislature that the people of Michigan want to decide -- for themselves -- what is best for them."

The prosecutor saw things differently. "This document, the words he wrote," Marlinga defended, "indicate that Dr. Kevorkian . . . in the final moments [of Hugh Gale's life] was substituting his own judgment for that of the patient."

Not so, cried attorney Schwartz. He charged that Marlinga's "spouting because he's seeking to appeal to certain political elements in what he hopes is his successful U.S. Senate campaign."

CORONER'S JURY SUMMONED

Marlinga was frustrated. Witnesses to Gale's suicide refused to cooperate and none would talk to police.

"I do not intend to gather that information by cutting newspaper clippings or gathering videotape from television stations," Marlinga explained. Instead, he ordered a coroner's inquest, a medieval procedure codified on Michigan's law books. The last such inquest in Macomb County was more than 50 years ago.

Like a grand jury, witnesses to Gale's last gasping words would be subpoenaed and, if necessary, ordered by a judge to testify. If any witness refused to testify but, instead, invoked the Fifth Amendment choosing to remain silent -- lest they incriminate themselves by their own testimony -- then the judge could grant them immunity from prosecution. Then, any reluctant witness would rest on the horns of a dilemma: either testify or go to jail for contempt of court.

The cavalcade of witnesses who would be given immunity from prosecution and forced to testify included widow Cheryl Gale, as well as Kevorkian-assistants Janus and Nicol. By the judge granting immunity (for any of these witnesses who took the Fifth Amendment and refused to testify), Marlinga would have tremendous leverage for extracting the facts from resistant witnesses: they would either testify or go straight to jail. This is how Marlinga planned to corner Kevorkian.

Marlinga seemed hungry for enough evidence to indict the doctor for manslaughter. "I'll go wherever the truth tells me to go," pledged Marlinga. Speculation was that he would call 15 or 16 witnesses, offering immunity to all, except Kevorkian! With everyone else's testimony, he hoped to corner and convict the doctor.

But Kevorkian's attorney Schwartz warned, "It's become more and more clear as this coroner's inquest goes on that it is something being put on by the prosecutor to satisfy his own personal and political agenda."

But would Kevorkian appear before the coroner's jury? "Sure, he'll be there, but only to call them scurrilous dogs," promised Fieger. "This is nothing more than an attempt to save Marlinga's political career," he scoffed. With that, a coroner's jury was summoned.

CHANCE ENCOUNTER

It was a chance encounter at the Gallery Restaurant in Southfield, Michigan the weekend before the coroner's inquest. As Marlinga looked up from his lunch, above the restaurant din, widow Cheryl Gale was dining with Janus, Nicol, Kevorkian and Fieger. "Of all the gin joints in all the bars in all the world, she'd have to come into mine," muttered Marlinga, repeating the line used by Rick at his American Cafe in *Casablanca*.

Cheryl Gale kept staring at Marlinga, exclaiming, "I know that man. I know that man."

Perhaps it was the politician in Marlinga that levitated him to approach Fieger, seeking leave to introduce himself to the widow Gale. Perhaps, Marlinga deeply felt her pain. In any event, Marlinga reached across the table to shake her hand apologizing, "I feel very sorry for you and I am sorry for this entire inquest, but I have a job to do."

This meeting "probably just took an edge off," reflects Marlinga. Before, "They didn't know me; I could have been a monster."

PLAYHOUSE OR COURTHOUSE?

The following Monday, Cheryl Gale went on the offensive. The widow Gale, represented by attorney

Fieger, launched a $10 million lawsuit against Oakland County Prosecutor Thompson and Right-to-Life advocate Lynn Mills. She accused them of conspiring to implicate her in her husband's death; she said they inflicted upon her extreme mental anguish and emotional distress.

Thompson charged that "Mr. Fieger is confusing the playhouse with the courthouse." Thompson accused that this lawsuit was "based purely on theatrics and fictions" saying that he would ". . .consider Mr. Fieger a mythomaniac."

Operation Rescue leader Lynn Mills was defiant, saying "I'm not going to back down." The self-described housewife concluded, "I don't know what they could take. . . .Can you get water out of a stone?"

INQUEST CONVENED

The inquest had been rolling along for nearly three hours. Assistants Janus and Nicol, as well as widow Cheryl Gale all refused to answer questions, invoking the Fifth Amendment against self-incrimination

Before refusing to testify, Kevorkian scoffed, "This is an inquisition, not an inquest. It's shameful for a blameless citizen to submit to an inquisition deceitfully called an inquest."Was Kevorkian invoking his Fifth Amendment right against self-incrimination? "I will not use the word *incriminate*," Kevorkian responded. "There's no way I can incriminate myself if I've done nothing illegal."

But, barely three hours after the inquisition circus had started, Marlinga, who had been waiting in the wings all along, burst into the courtroom to strike a surprise deal. In exchange for informal deposition testimony from Cheryl Gale, Marlinga abruptly moved that his request for an inquest be dismissed. All of the attorneys, laden by their briefcases in hand, sauntered out of the courtroom victorious.

The deal was this: Marlinga would take a deposition from Cheryl Gale and decide if Kevorkian should be charged with homicide for allegedly not removing Gale's mask when the dying man supposedly made a second request.

For the next month, Marlinga played "cat and mouse" with anxious reporters about his final decision. "I'm definitely leaning in the direction of not issuing charges," Marlinga teased. But, he mercilessly delayed his decision another three weeks.

Later, Marlinga explained, "I'm really not even looking for any conclusions, one way or another. I'm just puzzled or a little upset about why the physical evidence doesn't make sense. Before I close this whole thing out, I want everything to make sense."

Finally, weeks after Cheryl Gale's sworn deposition was given, Marlinga made a decision saying, "I believe Mrs. Gale when she says that her husband did not request to have the mask taken off a second time. I'm now satisfied there is not sufficient evidence in the document to go forward with charges."

In the end, U.S. Senate candidate Marlinga seemed to regret his involvement muttering, "It's a terrible thing to happen to me politically. It's very dangerous . . . an unfortunate thing to happen to me. Though Marlinga dropped out of that race for the U.S. Senate seat soon thereafter, his political ambitions did not wane."

chapter sixteen
Forty-Something

Martha Jane Ruwart, age 41 and single, used to work as a computer software engineer. After attending Michigan State University from 1972-1974, Ruwart ultimately received her computer science degree from San Diego State University. Recently, she moved from Cardiff-by-the-Sea, a small seaside resort near San Diego, California.

Ruwart was diagnosed with duodenal cancer in April 1992. Several therapies were unsuccessful in arresting this mortal, intestinal form of the disease. In December 1992, surgeons had operated on her. The cancer had spread unchecked to her ovaries and the odds of survival were deemed "very poor."

"She felt she had several more months of suffering that only would be followed by death," sister Mary Ruwart revealed. "She thought it was best to go when she was still lucid. . . . She had reached the end of her energy, was very tired and very much ready to go."

During her last three months Ruwart had stayed in Kalamazoo, Michigan with her three sisters, including Teresa Ruwart and Karen Swindler. All three sisters were to be with Ruwart when she died, as well as friends Gary and Brenda Fairfax, Lansing, Michigan.

"My sister had a very advanced cancer," recounted Mary Ruwart. "We've had a lot of cancer in our family. We've seen what it can do and the suffering it can cause."

Ruwart was to die by carbon monoxide, the method used in all but two of the 15 medicides thus far.

JONATHAN GRENZ

Jonathan Grenz, age 44, was single, had no children and lived alone. But it wasn't Michigan's weather that lured Grenz from the West Coast to the Frost Belt where Kevorkian practiced medicide.

The relatively young Grenz from Costa Mesa, California suffered from a virulent throat cancer that had started at the back of his tongue and had spread throughout his neck. Unable to work as a real estate agent for about a year, he had been diagnosed with cancer. Soon afterward, this fast-acting disease had forced surgeons to remove Jonathan's voice box and part of his neck.

"They cut his tongue out and, of course, he was shocked," said co-worker Linda Healey. "He had no idea the surgery would be so drastic and so severe. . . ."

To communicate, Grenz used an artificial larynx which creates a vibrating sound when applied to the neck, allowing Grenz to speak in a buzzing, manufactured voice.

After his operation in summer 1992, Jonathan could still walk, play blues guitar and drive the vehicles he repaired for a hobby. But by the end of that year, he was no longer able to eat or swallow, let alone leave his house or even exercise.

Then his mom died. "He was overwhelmed with grief," Healey suggested.

"I guess there's no reason to prolong any of this," Jonathan wrote. "I'm just not going to get any better and time goes by so slowly that it is unbearable.

"Life is not life anymore."

ANOTHER PHYSICIAN ATTENDS

Knowing the deadline was fast approaching, Jonathan had become more desperate, contacting Kevorkian out of fear and panic. Ultimately, Grenz himself foreclosed on the impending April Fool's Day ban on medicide.

Dr. Susan Grenz, Palm Harbor, Florida, a specialist in internal medicine, joined Kevorkian at the medicide of her brother. This was the first time another physician had witnessed a Kevorkian medicide.

Grenz was the third male whom Kevorkian would assist in medicide. Numerically, this finally put to rest previous criticisms that the suicide doctor preyed only on middle-aged women.

This was the fourth double suicide. As with Stanley Ball and Mary Biernat, neither Ruwart nor Grenz knew each other until shortly before dying. At Nicol's home in Waterford Township, Michigan, Ruwart and Grenz died on Thursday morning, February 18, 1993. Strangers in life, but companions in death, these two shared a tank of carbon monoxide.

At age 41, Ruwart was the youngest Kevorkian medicide patient to die thus far. On the living room sofa, she was the first of the pair to expire. Grenz was found in a bed in the back room.

Kevorkian was not particularly helpful to the Waterford Township police who arrived at the scene.

"We're not getting much cooperation because Dr. Kevorkian is waiting for his lawyer," griped Lieutenant Paul Vallad.

ONE CONTROVERSY REPLACES ANOTHER

Those opposed to Kevorkian launched a new attack, this time against The Procedure. Did Jack Kevorkian, M.D. properly assess the psychiatric state of the chronically-ill Grenz? Kevorkian had been rebuked before by critics similarly in the medicides of Majorie Wantz and Catherine Andreyev.

Grenz "was in a very depressed period of his life, it takes time to recover. . . .But he wasn't terminal," insisted Linda Healey, a co-worker of Grenz. "He was going through a time of crisis and looking for options."

Healey argued, "They never gave him a chance to grieve over his losses." She insisted that Kevorkian "didn't evaluate what John was going through."

Because another member of the medical profession had cooperated in these medicides, obitiatrist Kevorkian was swift to discard Healey's criticism as impertinent. "She's not a psychiatrist," Kevorkian scoffed.

Though as a medical doctor Kevorkian was trained in psychiatry to assess the competence of those who seek his assistance, Kevorkian's specialty was pathology.

In many instances, Kevorkian lacks the kind of intimate knowledge and longstanding relationship with his patients that some critics would prefer. Yet, if medicide were allowed to be practiced freely by doctors who so choose, including treating physicians, this criticism too would soon wane.

Referring to The Procedure, Kevorkian has written that a patient's "mental state is also of paramount importance, so a psychiatric evaluation is necessary and at least one psychiatrist must serve in this evaluation process."[59]

However, with Grenz, Kevorkian received no psychiatric reports. Instead, his decision to intervene was based on his own evaluation, a review of the medical records and extensive conversations with Grenz and his family.

Nobody asked Grenz to come to Michigan. He chose to do that on his own. Kevorkian determined that Grenz was making a knowledgeable, informed decision. After speaking with Grenz, Kevorkian was convinced there was no medical alternative.

Physicians routinely make many decisions that are ordinarily handed by psychiatrists. "I wonder whether Kevorkian has the luxury of psychiatrists willing to come forward to help him," questioned Dr. John Ravin, a psychiatrist from Torrence, California.

"On one hand, no one really wants to see the theatrics of Kevorkian," said Dr. Fred Whitehouse, an endocrinologist at Henry Ford Hospital. "But on the other hand, there's the patient out there who's suffering."

IMMEDIATE SUICIDE BAN

Until this double suicide, there had only been talk of accelerating the April 1st effective date of the ban on medicide. After Michigan's Governor John Engler signed the law in December banning assisted suicide, Kevorkian had assisted in seven deaths.

When the prohibition against assisted suicide became effective in 1993, private pollsters reported that 55 percent of those asked objected to this law banning assisted suicide; only 38 percent approved of the ban.

It was these two suicides, however, which provoked Right to Life and other critics to escalate their demands. They wanted the April Fool's Day ban on assisted suicide to be moved up -- immediately!

Doctors, who often prescribe pain pills to terminally ill patients, fretted that the new law may restrain them

213

from fully treating legitimate pain. Physicians lined up in Michigan to oppose the ban, whether its effective date were immediate or delayed. However, the Detroit-based Wayne County Medical Society, a division of the Michigan State Medical Society, adopted a resolution opposing the ban on assisted suicides.

LEGISLATIVE DIATRIBE

The ban on assisted suicide was made immediately effective and enacted into law by the Michigan House of Representatives (92-10). The Michigan Senate's debate produced the usual amount of invective aimed at Kevorkian.

Senator John F. Kelly, D-Grosse Pointe Woods, grandstanded with three floor speeches. Kelly -- himself an attorney -- castigated the doctor's lawyers as "mouthpieces." The Senator managed to brand Kevorkian as a "serial killer" three times, but was kind enough to diagnose him as a "psychopath" only once.

In a rare showing of bipartisan unity, Senator Doug Carl, R-Utica, highlighted Kevorkian as "Michigan's resident grim reaper." For those who had not kept score, Senator Carl enumerated, "Fifteen and counting -- that's the number of bodies that have assumed room temperature, thanks to Jack Kevorkian."

Expressing his concern about the quality of the rhetoric in this debate, Senator Vern Ellers, R-Grand Rapids, nonetheless, lashed out that Kevorkian had "the moral sensitivity of a moose." Senator Ellers went on to label Kevorkian "one gentleman who insists on, what I call, *Death by Press Conference.*"

When all senators were done posturing, the Michigan Senate voted (28-6) to make the ban on assisted suicide effective immediately.

Fieger deplored the immediate ban on medicide charging that "the Right to Life terrorist organization"

214

was responsible. He forewarned that legislators were trying to "codify the Bible. They're carrying out their precepts of religion and not the desires of the people who elected them. Clearly, if you have a vote of the people, it would go the other way."

Attorney Schwartz characterized this legislative action as "pretty stupid," charging it would make the Michigan legislature the "laughingstock of the nation:"

The legislature apparently seems to be in such a panic, such a tizzy that they can't even wait for the March 30 date. Why? Because of Dr. Kevorkian. It's clear this was aimed at him in the first place and that's what this is all about. It's embarrassing to have [such] a legislature.

Kevorkian, never at a loss for words, advised the Lansing government: "This is what [you lawmakers are] facing: . . .I break the law, my guns come out. Let's see if you can withstand it."

After the bravado and rhetoric, when all was said and done, the ban on assisted suicide took immediate effect at 5:00 p.m. on Thursday, February 25, 1993.

ACLU FILES LAWSUIT

A lawsuit was filed by the American Civil Liberties Union (ACLU) challenging the constitutionality of the Michigan law. The plaintiffs who sued included two cancer patients and a patient's friend plus six doctors and a pharmacist. The case was assigned to Wayne County Circuit Judge Cynthia D. Stephens.

Meanwhile, Fieger guaranteed, "Jack will hold off." The obitiatrist would make no more house calls until the court ruled on a preliminary injunction.

"I'm pleasantly amazed," beamed ACLU attorney Elizabeth Gleicher. "I think it's very responsible [of Dr. Kevorkian to hold off]. People *should* have faith in the legal system." Gleicher argued that chronically ill patients "have a right to determine under our Constitution what they can do to their body."

Attorney Howard Simon of ACLU's Michigan Chapter cautioned, "We're trying to distance ourselves from Kevorkian. I've never spoken with him. I've had no contact with him. Our case stands totally independent of Kevorkian."

That was just fine with Jack Kevorkian who was not a plaintiff in this lawsuit. "I don't care whether they appeal the law or not. Let them distance themselves from me," Kevorkian said brashly. "I don't need the ACLU's help."

chapter seventeen

Loopholes in the Law

J udge Cynthia Stephens had been expected to rule on a particular Friday but, instead, she was out of town for the weekend. The new Michigan law -- prohibiting assisting suicides -- remained on the books, threatening a felony conviction, up to four years in prison and a $2,000 fine. Kevorkian had promised to schedule no more medicides until after the court had ruled. But Death's Impresario was impatient and time waits for no one.

At 10:30 a.m. Sunday morning when Ronald Mansur died, no family members were present. No presuicide videotape was shot. No records were made by any attending obitiatrist . . . and certainly none were left lying in the trash this time for Lynn Mills to scavenge. No scrawled suicide note was left behind by the patient. No press conference was convened.

Kevorkian was mute when he emerged from the building where Ronald Mansur had committed suicide.

"He will not tell us what happened inside the building," criticized Detroit Police Inspector Gerald Stewart.

Oakland County Prosecutor Thompson, though out of his jurisdiction, gratuitously observed, "He's basically thumbed his nose at law enforcement, in part, because he feels he has public support."

When police arrived, Mansur was dead and all that could be said of Kevorkian was that he may have been present. Nonetheless, said Inspector Stewart, "our job is to determine whether the suicide was assisted."

But Kevorkian had police and prosecutors off-balance. Police were compelled to establish who, *if anyone*, assisted the 54 year old Mansur. Meanwhile, Kevorkian remained a law unto himself, seemingly unstoppable. "If the evidence is there, we'll bring charges," Inspector Stewart promised but "if not . . . we will not."

There was an uncharacteristic lack of details surrounding Mansur's suicide. Yes, Kevorkian was in the building and so was Mansur. But now Mansur was dead and Kevorkian wasn't talking. Otherwise, what was the evidence against Kevorkian?

Authorities speculate that Kevorkian may have attended Mansur's suicide and, if so, that may have made Mansur Dr. Kevorkian's sixteenth medicide patient. The mask over Mansur's face led to two canisters stamped CARBON MONOXIDE. From the deadly tanks led a string, tied to the middle finger of Mansur's left hand; the string was attached to a paper clip that had crimped the flow of the poison gas.

"I know that when he put that mask on his face, he had his finger sticking up in the air as if to say, *'Screw you all for the laws that made me suffer like this,'*" interpreted his friend of 14 years, Donna Cady of Novi, Michigan.

Loopholes in the Law

When Mansur died, he was wearing slippers and enshrouded in a white-knit blanket. He died while slumped in a reclining chair in his family's real estate agency office on Detroit's east side.

The business office was nestled among dilapidated brick and drab cinder block buildings. Peeling paint and steel bars guarded doors and windows, but they were not enough to keep Dr. Death out.

Mansur was a kind man and maintained a large number of rental income properties. He was shrewd but if you were a tenant who could not always pay the rent on time, Mansur might be the one to give you a break.

When he first started out in the real estate business, "Ronnie Mansur was a bit of a playboy, flashy dresser, drove around in a Cadillac and considered himself a real *ladies man*," recalled attorney Victor A. Gold. "He was likeable, friendly and seemed quite successful."

Now divorced with a daughter, real estate broker Mansur had grown terminally ill, suffering months of excruciating bone and lung cancer that had metasticized. He had gone through chemotherapy and begun to lose his hair; his body was emaciated, his skin had turned yellow-green.

"He was in hell," relayed Cady. "He would cry on the phone." Mansur's morphine pump was strapped to his belt; attending him like a friend, only the pump could relieve the pain. But in recently months, Mansur had markedly declined.

"He had to have a nurse drive him to work," Tony Arnold reported. "I offered him a smoke and he said 'No,' that he had bone cancer and he couldn't smoke cigarettes anymore." Two years ago, this muscular fitness buff and health enthusiast had been diagnosed with cancer. At first, he had a painful knob on his knee. His daily vitamin regimen and health spa workouts could not forestall the inevitable.

"He started off walking with a cane, then two canes," remembered Errick Wilson. "And every step he took, you could see the pain in his face. He had all kinds of medicines, but it wasn't doing any good."

The bitter irony was that this same disease had killed his father. Once-upbeat, Mansur had begun to ail, grew unhappy and turned profoundly inward.

"The last couple of months he was real depressed, real edgy. Here his father had just died of cancer," Wilson reported.

Neighbor Cornelius Clay remembers the good things: "That man was like my father. He was just good to me. If I needed some change or something, I could go in there and get it. He'd say, '*Get a job*,' but he didn't worry me about paying him back. Those Mansurs were good people."

DON'T EVEN TRY TO PROSECUTE

A lone male caller telephoned 911 at 10:30 a.m. to report the death of Mansur. At the scene, the only "evidence" against Kevorkian was his physical presence in a building where Mansur was found to have committed suicide; nonetheless, Kevorkian was arrested and ordered to Detroit Police headquarters to be fingerprinted and questioned. His attorney drove him to the police department.

"The people of the state of Michigan will not allow him to be prosecuted. Don't even try to prosecute Kevorkian. Don't even try," warned Fieger. "It's not a crime to be present when someone commits suicide. If the prosecutor wants to have a three-ring circus in [criminal] court while I kick their butts around the block, I'm ready."

Police wanted to know: Who obtained the tanks? Were the tanks operable without Kevorkian's assistance? Who bought the carbon monoxide? How did the two men get to the real estate office, since Mansur couldn't drive and Kevorkian owned no car? Who procured the mask and tubes? Did Mansur pull on the mask himself? Who turned on the gas?

To be frank, Detroit Police knew that anyone could have provided the poison carbon monoxide gas, available at many medical supply stores. Michigan had no laws preventing purchase of the lethal substance. "Anyone can call us up and say they want a mixture that has [oxygen and] carbon monoxide, because it's not a regulated gas," explained Brian Hickey of Airco Gases in Ann Arbor. If "they've got a use for it, if they've got good credit, we can do business."

However, during their two hours at police headquarters, Kevorkian and his attorney refused to answer such questions. The pair spent most of their time glued to the television set, watching the Knicks-Hornets basketball playoffs. Then without ever criminally charging Kevorkian, Detroit Police released him to his attorney's custody.

All along, Kevorkian contended he did nothing illegal. A friend of Mansur stepped forward to explain. "Ron had a plan to do this himself and did do it himself," reported Cady. He had planned this without Kevorkian. He had wanted to do this in January," Cady explained. "He wanted to have done it before the law took effect but he was not able to reach Dr. Kevorkian and make arrangements."

Though Kevorkian was in the building where police discovered Mansur's body, no direct evidence implicated him in assisting Mansur's suicide -- other than his physical presence at the death scene. There was no Michigan law against observing a suicide.

"The problem is they have no way of proving it," Wayne State University Law School professor Robert Sedler smiled sardonically. "The person is dead and there are no other witnesses, so nobody knows what Kevorkian did."

Apparently, Doctor Death had slipped through the noose which Michigan lawmakers had tried so hard to tighten around his neck.

WHEELS OF JUSTICE

For the next several days while Detroit Police were questioning Kevorkian's role, Judge Stephens was churning out her legal opinion on the constitutionality of the ban against assisted suicide.

Impatiently awaiting Judge Stephens' decision, Fieger was chafing at the bit demanding, "Let's get it on. Let's just start kicking some butt in court. Let's have the Scopes [monkey] trial here." In 1925, Charles Darwin's teachings on the theory of evolution in a Tennessee public school were put on trial. "Let's have the biggest trial in United States history and weigh our side against all the religious fanatics," Fieger urged. "That will be interesting because this is boring to talk about who did what, when, where."

On the Thursday after Mansur killed himself, Detroit Police raided Kevorkian's Royal Oak apartment. They took a cardboard box and some plastic tubing. "Maybe they got some paper clips," Fieger gibed.

When the raid was done, Detroit Police Lieutenant Tommie Alston excused himself by saying, "We're just investigating. Presence [at a suicide] is not assistance."

RIGHT TO DIE

As the week wound to a close, Judge Stephens ruled on the Michigan law which had, until then, banned assisting a suicide. "This court cannot envisage a more fundamental right than the right to self-determination. The court finds that the right of self-determination . . .

includes the right to choose to cease living." Ultimately though, the judge rejected the new law banning assisted-suicide on dry, procedural grounds.

After the ruling, Fieger moaned, "Now we'll have no opportunity to have a circus trial where we'll be able to respond to the reactionary forces led by Governor Engler and expose them for the fraud that they are."

After Judge Stephens declared the ban against assisted suicide unconstitutional, Inspector Gerald Stewart determined, "We are no longer pursuing the case. Our investigation has ceased." Medicide, at least then, had become unpunishable.

The court issued an injunction forcing authorities to stop prosecuting Kevorkian for assisting with suicides. The Michigan attorney general has appealed the judge's ruling.

The Michigan Court of Appeals subsequently reversed the circuit court and reinstated the ban on assisted suicide pending further circuit court proceedings on the ACLU initiated litigation. Assisting a suicide remained unlawful in Michigan, while both the public and prosecutors awaited Dr. Kevorkian's next move.

chapter eighteen

Death Takes No Holiday

By early August, pundits were suggesting that Dr.
Death had taken a holiday. Kevorkian had not been
associated with any assisted suicides for several months.
In his obitiatry practice over the past three years, Dr.
Death traditionally has taken a summer vacation.

During one weekend at the end of July 1993,
Kevorkian had been a guest at the home of Schwartz,
one of his attorneys. Together they played ping pong.
"He's really very good at it," beamed Schwartz.

While this was Dr. Death's longest holiday from his
practice of obitiatry, it was not from any dearth of patients. Hundreds of people had contacted Kevorkian
seeking his assistance to end their lives though few were
eligible under Kevorkian's strict procedure. Though Dr.
Death had taken a brief holiday, the hiatus was soon to
end.

DR. DEATH

LOU GEHRIG'S LEGACY

Thomas W. Hyde, Jr., 30, was in tip-top shape, robust, and looking ahead to a bright future. Vigorous and vibrant, when he was not working in construction and landscaping, Hyde was the strapping woodsman who liked to ski, fish and hunt. Hyde lived with his fiancée, Heidi Fernandez, 35, and their 18-month old daughter, Carmen Denise Fernandez. He also had a 12 year old son, Joe, from a prior marriage.

In the summer of 1992, Hyde visited Botsford Hospital complaining of muscular weakness even though he had the physique of a weight lifter. Within weeks, his muscles began to twitch and his speech slurred. Hyde was devastated to hear that he was diagnosed with amyotrophic lateral sclerosis (ALS), called Lou Gehrig's disease: no known cause, no known cure. Several thousand victims in the United States are stricken with Lou Gehrig's disease named after the famed New York Yankee who died of the degenerative neuromuscular disorder.

Hyde then began regular group therapy sessions at the Michigan Institute for Neurological Disorders, a muscular dystrophy/ALS clinic in Farmington Hills, Michigan. Hyde's neurologist, Dr. Louis Rentz, characterized Hyde as "coping, but very, very unhappy. He had a nice life with a lot of prospects going for him when his ALS disease started, but I think he felt very stricken."

Hyde had always been such a physical person, never thinking that his body would turn against him. However, by Thanksgiving, it took him nearly 20 minutes to inch his way up three flights of stairs.

In less than one year after the initial diagnosis of ALS, Hyde's disease was declared terminal; doctors projected that Hyde, perhaps, had another year to live. In a crudely scrawled note attached to his back door, Hyde

226

protested, "As much as anything, I want to be free and enjoy...."

Hyde recently had moved from Florida to live in Novi, Michigan taking up residence in an apartment complex in this solid, blue collar suburb of Detroit with Fernandez and their daughter Carmen. Hyde's apartment was handicap accessible.

"When they first moved in here," neighbor David VanGelder recalls, "he was on a walker and, as time progressed, he was more in a wheel chair." Hyde was frustrated by his inability to fight this disease.

MILLER'S TALE

Even in its so-called mild form, ALS imprisons its victims in their own private jail cell. "You lose your balance, or you catch your toe, and all of a sudden, you're picking yourself up off of the ground," reports ALS-victim Michael Miller, St. Clair Shores, Michigan. Your mind stays alert but you are held captive by a failing body.

Though confined to a wheel chair, Miller's case of ALS was unique and differed from that of Hyde. In fact, Miller's irrevocable though post-dated death notice was delivered by ALS when he was only 25 years old. Doctors were too quick to shortchange Miller when they awarded him only three years to live. That was 24 years ago.

Nonetheless, Miller empathized with Hyde cautioning, "You can't second guess someone with a terminal illness. They know -- and only they know -- how much they can take." Indeed, Miller had drawn his own line in the sand if his disease worsened.

Imprisoned in his own electric wheel chair, a cellular phone within finger's reach, Miller stressed, "It's not my choice to live dependent on a machine." When he required a machine to breath for him, then Miller wanted to die. And if Miller found himself in Hyde's situation, he hoped that Dr. Kevorkian would be there to assist him.

CHILLING REALIZATION

Over a Christmas holiday weekend in 1992, Hyde's sister, Michelle Hyde, had taken both families to the tropical island of Bimini. "I figured it would be the last time I would see Tommy alive," Michelle said, justifying the extravagance. She shared a snapshot of Hyde standing on a white sand beach, gazing wistfully into a jaded ocean, propping himself up on a walking stick. "We had a good time," Michelle remembered.

By May 1993, while Hyde always loved to be outside, he was confined to his motorized wheelchair driving along the sidewalks around the apartment complex or inching along with the aid of a walker.

Since his diagnosis the previous summer, Hyde had come to some terrible realizations. In a letter to his ex-wife, Laurie Erdody, the mother and custodial parent of Joe, their 12 year old son, he wrote:

I'm unsure how to begin this.... Carmen refuses to come near because I can't pick her up and hold her or get her off the floor and play with her and that too hurts.

I want Joe to remember the way I was, not to remember what I have become. It is nearly impossible for me to communicate with him. At times, if I fall or am having a bad day and start to tremor uncontrollably, there is a look of fear and pity in his eyes, and that hurts. I don't want him to see me like this. He doesn't need memories of that.

While ALS normally weakens the body slowly, a few victims have lived decades with mild forms. Yet, Hyde's decline in health was swift. "Thomas Hyde's disease had taken a rapidly progressive course. He was barely able to speak, let alone swallow his own saliva; when he coughed, he choked; he couldn't eat and had almost no muscular movement," reported his neurologist, Dr. Rentz.

He had everything going for him and then, all of a sudden, it was taken away. He realized that he was not going to get better. He knew that he was rapidly getting worse. He wanted so to enjoy his child and his family, but unfortunately he could not. Hyde was profoundly depressed.

In its terminal phase, ALS is hideous: feeding tubes, respirators and, inevitably, choking to death on your own spit while conscious. This was an end that Hyde did not want. Hyde recalled that in December 1992, Dr. Kevorkian had assisted another ALS patient, Marguerite Tate, with her suicide. Racked by the same disease, Hyde never expected to see his 31st birthday in October 1993.

Neighbor Carl Gibboney readily offered that Hyde "seemed kind of hunched over. He didn't seem to be very strong. But he never seemed to me to be in that bad of shape."

Another neighbor, Denise MacKenzie, related, "I thought of coming up to him just to say *hello* because he looked a little bit sad one day and was just gazing out at the pond. I thought maybe I should say something ... but I never did."

THE QUIET DECISION

"I've seen a lot of patients in the same state as Hyde," said his physician, Dr. Rentz. "They look at what they *can't* do instead of what they *can* do. He could see his wife. He could see his daughter, Carmen. There were elements of life he could enjoy and he was not in pain."

Hyde was having trouble with his health insurance. Concerns about medical bills added to his frustrations. Privately, Hyde had contemplated suicide ever since he was stricken with ALS. Perhaps because Dr. Rentz adamantly opposed physician-assisted medicide, Hyde never confided in his own treating physician his decision to seek treatment with Dr. Death. "He never mentioned it to anyone at the clinic," Rentz remembered, "even though he was close to a lot of people."

Hyde confided his plans to commit suicide to, perhaps, only four people: Fernandez (his fiancée); Erdody (his ex-wife) and their son, Joe; and Michelle Hyde (his sister).

Hyde told Fernandez very clearly that he wanted and needed to die. By then, Hyde had intense pain, could hardly swallow, and was using every bit of energy just to breathe; when lying in bed, he would have to be turned on his side to help him breathe. He communicated with others by scrawling with a dry marker on a legal pad. During the last year, he would become evil with wild mood swings. Though Fernandez was nursing his every need, Hyde once screamed at her, "You're not doing anything for me."

By consulting with Dr. Kevorkian, Fernandez believed that Hyde was doing the right thing, was doing what he wanted to do. She maintained that Hyde's soul needed to be released from a body that had broken down, a body that was not working anymore, a body that was incapable of doing what Hyde, in his mind, said it should do.

Hyde's surrender was obvious to Fernandez when he could no longer help care for their 18-month old baby, Carmen. Watching the infant splash about in her swimming pool, the girl suddenly climbed out and dashed toward the road. Immobile, Hyde could only watch in fright and grip the horn on his wheel chair to warn the child's mother.

On Thursday, July 29, 1993, Hyde confided to Erdody, "I am not living. I'm only existing and it's an existence in hell." Erdody concedes that when her ex-husband "realized there was nothing they could do, he just gave up emotionally." As for their own 12 year old son, Joe, Erdody explained, "It wasn't that he was for it ... but Joe understood the reasons behind it."

The next day, Hyde telephoned his sister, Michelle, in Ft. Lauderdale, Florida. Hyde told his sister about the impending medicide. "I just wanted him to be happy and he wasn't happy anymore," Michelle said. She immediately left by plane for Michigan to be with her brother.

BELLE ISLE

Very early Wednesday morning, August 4, 1993, Fernandez rolled Hyde out for his ride to meet Dr. Death. He was smiling, happy. "I love you, Babe," Hyde assured Fernandez. "Please take care of my little girl. I love her very much." At age 30, Hyde was to be Kevorkian's youngest patient so far.

This was one of the prettiest summer mornings ever on Belle Isle, a favorite refuge from the city for Detroiters. The oblong island, a mile wide and three miles long, is nature's gem planted in the middle of emerald, shimmering waters. Downbound freighters plowed through the Detroit River along the St. Lawrence Seaway to the Atlantic Ocean while hundreds of deer roam freely in the thick woods offshore.

Not long after sunrise, Kevorkian drove Hyde across the chalk white bridge spanning two dozen granite arches. The pair bumped along in Kevorkian's still rust-

231

ing, quarter-century-old VW camper bus with its engine rattling like a bucket of loose spoons and its muffler puttering. Kevorkian's first medicide patient, Janet Adkins, had made her final exit in this same camper by pushing the switch on Kevorkian's experimental death machine, the Mercitron. Tan curtains (new only three years ago for Adkins' medicide) still fully blanked the camper windows.

On the advice of lawyers, family members and loved ones were constrained by Michigan's ban against assisting a suicide from joining Hyde on Belle Isle where he was to end his own life. Though they desired to be with Hyde, they were justifiably fearful of being prosecuted under Michigan's vague statutory ban against assisting a suicide.

Because Kevorkian's medical licenses had been suspended, the Mercitron was mothballed because the device required three different prescription drugs. For today, Kevorkian had purchased from his own funds a mixture of carbon monoxide and oxygen, compressed into a gas-grill style canister. Along with some tubing and a face mask, Kevorkian was well equipped to assist Hyde in committing suicide.

On a serene, interior road near the woods, between the zoo and nature center, while elsewhere the mad dash of morning commuters crammed Detroit's freeways with rush hour traffic, Kevorkian calmly parked his ancient camper.

Shortly before 8:00 a.m., Dr. Death placed a mask over the face of Thomas Hyde. Kevorkian used a paper clip to crimp the tubing which connected the face mask to the canister of gas. A loose string ran from the paper clip to Hyde's left hand. Hyde had barely enough movement in his left hand to pull the clip which would uncrimp the tubing, allowing the carbon monoxide to rush to his face mask. Kevorkian turned on the flow of

232

poison gases. When everything was ready, Hyde himself pulled the string, removing the paper clip and triggering the release of deadly gas to his mask.

After Hyde expired, Kevorkian telephoned Heidi Fernandez, and then summoned his attorney to the island. An anonymous telephone call was made to police reporting the medicide.

DETAINED FOR QUESTIONING

When Fieger arrived on Belle Isle, he drove directly to the Tudor-style police station with its charming fieldstone facade. As Fieger entered the police post, the commanding officer (who had long thought he owned Belle Isle) instantly recognized him exclaiming, "Oh, no, now what has Kevorkian gone and done on my island?" Fieger assured the commander that Dr. Death was in his park.

Following Fieger, the commanding officer drove toward where Kevorkian's VW camper was expected to be, but he wasn't there. As Fieger and the Detroit police commander scouted Belle Isle, they spotted Kevorkian's van chugging along. Apparently, Dr. Death had become impatient waiting and was driving himself directly to the police station. The body of Thomas Hyde rode along in the back of the camper next to tanks of carbon monoxide.

The commander in his marked patrol car pulled up behind Kevorkian's VW bus, activating his flashing lights, barking orders over the loud speaker to "pull it over, doctor." As directed, Kevorkian drove his van to the secluded parking lot at the rear of the Belle Isle police mini-station, with Fieger shadowing in his vehicle. The Wayne County Medical Examiner dispatched a van to remove the body of Kevorkian's 17th medicide patient since 1990.

DR. DEATH

In less than an hour, a plain clothes detective commandeered Kevorkian's camper and left in a convoy, sandwiched between two marked patrol cars. The trademark VW van headed downtown to Detroit Police headquarters.

Meanwhile, Fernandez made the necessary pilgrimage to the Wayne County morgue to identify Hyde's body. After an autopsy, Hyde's remains would be released to Fernandez for cremation.

At police headquarters, Wayne County Prosecutor John O'Hair confronted Kevorkian and dared, "If you are genuinely interested in challenging the assisted suicide law, it would be more forthcoming if you admitted your involvement." Kevorkian listened and thought.

Though detained for some six hours and questioned by homicide detectives, Jack Kevorkian was not arrested. About 3:00 p.m., he was released.

STARTLING ADMISSION

Upon being released, Kevorkian and Fieger immediately convened a news conference. Fernandez was casually dressed totally in white -- baseball cap, tee shirt, shorts and tennis shoes -- standing behind Kevorkian as an expression of support. Kevorkian wasted no time in thrashing the medical establishment:

They're politicians first, businessmen second and physicians third. They ought to be ashamed of themselves to have human beings, like Thomas Hyde, suffer immensely, unable to move any muscle, cannot speak, cannot swallow, have pain and, in addition to all that, they turn their heads to say, "We've got to discuss this a little more."

All they need say is, "This is a needed medical service. This is how we will do it. We don't need any law to tell us how to do this, just like we don't need any law to tell us how to do a heart transplant or a gall bladder operation. This is our business. We know it." And this has nothing to do with religion, philosophy or ethics; it has to do with medical service.

The world knows there's a need for this. The talk is senseless, pointless; there's nothing new to be said about this.

Detailing the need for assisted suicide, Kevorkian explained passionately that "Some patients can't move. They need help. They can't do it themselves. They can't pull a pin, they can't push a button. So the doctor has to do it like they do in the Netherlands."

This was the second suicide that Kevorkian had attended since Michigan made it illegal to assist a suicide; both had occurred in the City of Detroit. Defiant and dressed in a white shirt and tie, with TV cameras and news microphones whirling, Kevorkian flatly admitted his role in that morning's death of Thomas Hyde:

I assisted Thomas Hyde in a merciful suicide. There's no doubt about that. I state it emphatically. I will always do so when a patient needs it because I am a physician.

Kevorkian was a little cagey about the details. Detroit Police Inspector Gerald Stewart lamented, "He didn't go far enough for us to charge him" based on these comments alone.

Equally so, after hearing this admission by Kevorkian, the prosecutor wasn't fully satisfied. O'Hair was telling reporters that, if he could prove that Kevorkian provided the means for Hyde to end his own life, he *probably* would prosecute.

LINE IN THE SAND

In 1988, O'Hair extracted a guilty plea from Dr. Donald Caraccio for injecting potassium chloride into a terminally-ill patient; the doctor served five years probation. But two years later, O'Hair lost a case against Bertram "Bob" Harper for assisting his cancer-stricken wife, Virginia "Ginny" Harper, in her suicide after the couple traveled from California to Michigan, laboring under the misimpression that assisted suicide would not be prosecuted.

The morning after Hyde's death, O'Hair went live on local radio station WJR, calling Kevorkian's bluff by demanding a confession before he would charge Kevorkian. Asked to spell out his requirements for prosecution, O'Hair said he would like Kevorkian to "say the magic words" detailing Hyde's death, such as "I, Jack Kevorkian, turned the gas on knowing Mr. Hyde wanted to cause his own death" or "I provided the means knowing that Mr. Hyde was going to use this equipment to cause his own death."

Kevorkian readily promised to be a cooperative criminal suspect. "I want to do everything possible to make O'Hair's job easier," Kevorkian said.

"Good," O'Hair responded. "I'll wait and see what happens and then we'll go from there."

Within hours after O'Hair made his radio request to hear Kevorkian "say the magic words," the bespectacled obitiatrist donned his sky-blue suit, white shirt and tie to appear at his second news conference in as many days. By now, TV cameras had become familiar props in his attorneys' conference room. As the cameras rolled, Kevorkian tailored an unprecedented and dramatic confession directly aimed at Prosecutor O'Hair. Kevorkian spelled out his role to the media:

I supplied the van which was my personal van. At no time was there anyone else in the van beside me and Mr. Hyde. I drove Hyde to Belle Isle.

I supplied the [poisonous carbon monoxide] gas. I supplied the tubing, the mask and all the necessary equipment. I connected the tubing to the tank. I put the clip on the tubing. I put the mask over on Mr. Hyde's face because he could not move that much; he could barely move his left hand, his left forearm and he could not even extend his fingers. His fingers were almost in a fixed position. He could not move them very much at all. I put the clip on the tubing to obstruct flow. I turned on the gas by the main valve on the tank.

I asked him one more time if he was sure what he was doing. I could not get an intelligible reply, but there was a small smile and you could see him crack his lips. He looked up with sort of a pleasant face, pleasant eyes and a moan or two and I thought I heard him say, "I'm fine."

Then I decided to go ahead. I instructed him that all he had to do was move his left fore-

arm a bit and pull. He then pulled the string
and the clip came off the tubing. It was a
slow flow of gas, very slow volume. He then
went on and died.

Standing up to be counted, Kevorkian handed O'Hair
the keys to his own prosecution, hoping his confession
was enough to be arrested and charged with the crime
of assisting in Hyde's suicide. Having forced matters to
a head and put his life on the line, Kevorkian promised
O'Hair to surrender any other evidence he might need
to press criminal charges.

Kevorkian also repeated his vow to go on a hunger
strike if jailed. "I don't want to be a martyr. It's silly.
It's rather kind of childish," Kevorkian explained. "But
I do not choose to live in a society that's still in the
dark ages. Now if the civilized world endorses as a law
and makes it a crime to continue the agony of people
like Thomas Hyde, then I don't want to live in that kind
of a society."

Confidently Fieger said, "I expect that Prosecutor
O'Hair will do exactly what he said he would do. He
will allow the evidence to be analyzed, the autopsy to
be completed and fingerprints to be taken. Dr.
Kevorkian has provided the evidence that he asked for
and I would expect that there would be a warrant issued for Dr. Kevorkian's arrest and prosecution by next
week."

O'Hair had drawn a line in the sand and, undaunted,
Kevorkian had plowed right through it.

DEFENSE PREDICTIONS

"Laws that are contrary to the will of the people and
contrary to the morality of the people will not be enforced by the people," Fieger certified at a news conference.

"In 1993, a jury of Dr. Kevorkian's peers is not going to send him to prison for assisting a terminally ill, suffering human being who carried out a last volitional act of self-determination," predicted Fieger.

"Laws that are unjust, laws that make people suffer will not be enforced. This law doesn't do anything to Dr. Kevorkian. It makes Thomas Hyde suffer. If this law were enforced against Thomas Hyde, all it would do is make his doctor put feeding tubes in him so that he could breathe and be fed like that. No juror is going to enforce such a law.

"We executed the Nazis in 1946 and 1947 for rigidly following their own laws. Who will imprison Dr. Kevorkian for refusing to follow a law that makes people suffer?" Fieger asked. "Jurors will recognize they are in need of Dr. Kevorkian's services and that this law will make them suffer also!"

"If this law is enforced, it prevents Thomas Hyde from consulting a physician to end his life peaceably. His life was going to end hideously in the face of this disease. Thomas Hyde was only seeking a doctor's help in having a peaceful, soft landing out of this world. That's a terrible law and Dr. Kevorkian will win because he's right," predicted Fieger.

"The time has come for the people of the state of Michigan to know they either have a right to decide their own well-being, or they don't," decreed attorney Fieger. "This law is not directed at Dr. Kevorkian, it's directed at Thomas Hyde and it's directed at you and me."

Fieger knew that O'Hair had all of the TV tape and could show it to the jury. "But he's still going to lose," chided Fieger who predicted prosecutors would never get a jury to convict Jack Kevorkian. "Not with me representing him, they won't!"

FAMILY MESSAGE

The day after Hyde's medicide, his family stepped forward to express their gratitude to Dr. Kevorkian. "Thank you," said Michelle Hyde between sobs. "All I can say is —thank you for helping Tommy because he's better off where he is now."

As for young Joe, the lad could only smile awkwardly as his mother explained, "He's having a very hard time, but he knows that his father is in a better place and things are much easier for him now."

Tom Hyde remained an outdoorsman until he made his final exit near the wooded trails on Belle Isle. Erdody smiled through her tears, satisfied that "Now, at last, Tom can walk again in the woods . . . just as he always liked to do."

To be sure, Hyde hoped for a private wake, but not one that would be melancholy, please. "I want it to be outside," Hyde said and "I want everybody to have a good time, drink beer and wear shorts."

PICKING UP THE PIECES

Before sunset on the day of Hyde's medicide, the Home Care medical equipment company had arrived at his apartment. Efficiently, Dr. Rentz had ordered the pick-up of Hyde's wheelchair and seat belt.

Michigan Senator Robert Geake (D-Northville) who helped write the criminal law against assisting a suicide observed, ". . . I am disappointed. Kevorkian wants to test the law: Kevorkian believes he is right and the Michigan legislature is wrong."

But Michigan Governor Engler charged, "If *Mr. Kevorkian* assisted in a suicide, the law ought to be enforced."

Prosecutor O'Hair reluctantly pressed criminal charges for assisting Hyde commit suicide. If convicted

240

of this felony, Kevorkian would face up to four years in prison and $2,000 in fines. However, O'Hair pledged not to seek jail time if Kevorkian were convicted; while waiting trial Kevorkian was free on a $100,000 no-cash personal bond.

On Thursday, September 9, District Judge Willie G. Lipscomb called Kevorkian a "very courageous person" and reflected, "It would be very difficult for many of us to say there isn't some right [affecting] how we can leave" this Earth. But constrained by the law, after a preliminary examination, Judge Lipscomb ordered Kevorkian to stand trial.

THE 18th MEDICIDE

·Hours after being released by Judge Lipscomb, Kevorkian made his 18th house call, this time attending to Donald O'Keefe, 73, a retired machine repairman at Ford Motor Co. About 10:00 p.m., O'Keefe took his own life with the chief practitioner of assisted suicide in attendance.

O'Keefe died in his small brick bungalow in Redford Township. Deteriorating from bone cancer, O'Keefe would scream out from pain. O'Keefe could not be moved and his physician reportedly would not come to him; only Dr. Death would make a house call to alleviate O'Keefe's interminable pain.

Prosecutor O'Hair prosecuted Kevorkian for O'Keefe's suicide. Not bothered by prison, Kevorkian, 65, pledged to continue his civil disobedience, quoting Henry David Thoreau who said: "The only place of honor for such a man is in prison."

Epilogue

Jack Kevorkian has no desire to be rich or famous. He doesn't eat much. He lives in a monastic cubicle, in a walk-up apartment in downtown Royal Oak, Michigan -- *Our Town USA*. He has scant possessions and few friends. He is now without a vehicle. Existing on Social Security plus some slight savings, many have invited him on a speaking tour where, on the circuit, he could earn $10,000 or more per talk. He won't do it.

Kevorkian has allowed many to confront the challenge of assisted suicide.

Kevorkian has allowed many to confront the challenge of assisted suicide. There have been 16 medicides so far connected to Jack Kevorkian. There have been over 100 family members. If the doctor had done something wrong, why has not one family member said he killed?

For those with such terrible suffering that it has stolen all quality of life, Kevorkian has been there to assist in concluding what, by then, has most regrettably become a miserable existence.

Kevorkian has felled a monolith in society. He has not embraced the right to die so much as he has championed an individual's choice to terminate their own agony. Kevorkian proclaims, ". . .a person's right to life or death, the choice about death, is entirely a personal decision. . . ."

To those who have elected the goodness of planned death, Kevorkian will be remembered not as *Dr. Death*, but as *Dr. Life*.

TABLE A

STATE LAWS AFFECTING ASSISTED SUICIDE

May, 1993

Assisted Suicide a Crime
or
Legislation Pending to make it a crime

Alaska	Nebraska
Arkansas	*North Carolina* *
Arizona	North Dakota
California	New Hampshire
Colorado	New Jersey
Connecticut *	New Mexico
Delaware	New York
Florida	*Ohio* *
Georgia *	Oklahoma
Illinois *	Oregon
Indiana *	Pennsylvania
Kansas	*South Carolina* *
Maine	South Dakota
Michigan	*Tennessee* *
Minnesota	*Texas* *
Mississippi	Washington
Missouri	*Wisconsin* *
Montana	

Information appearing in Table A courtesy of The Hemlock Society U.S.A., Eugene, Oregon.

Endnotes

1. Kevorkian, J. "The Last Fearsome Taboo: Medical Aspects of Planned Death." *Medicine and Law* (1988) 7:10-11.

2. Kevorkian, J. "Cerebral Blood Circulation and Brain Death." *Western Journal of Medicine* (1988) Jul 149(1):94.

3. Kevorkian, J. "Marketing of Human Organs and Tissues Is Justified and Necessary." *Medicine and Law* (1989) 7:564.

4. Kevorkian, J. "A Fail-Safe Model for Justifiable Medically-Assisted Suicide." *American Journal of Forensic Psychiatry* (1992) Vol. 13, No. 1, p. 17.

5. Kevorkian, J., M.D. *Prescription: Medicide — The Goodness of Planned Death.* Prometheus Books (Buffalo, NY 1991), p. 160.

6. Kevorkian, J. "A Comprehensive Bioethical Code for Medical Exploitation of Humans Facing Imminent and Unavoidable Death." *Medicine and Law* (1986) 5:186.

7. Kevorkian, J. *Canadian Medical Association Journal,* Vol. 136, 15 Jun 1987, p. 1240.

8. Kevorkian, *Prescription: Medicide,* p. 43.

9. *Journal of Criminal Law, Criminology, and Police Science,* June, 1959.

10. Kevorkian, J. "Our Unforgivable Trespass." *Clinical Pediatrics* (1966) Vol. 5, No. 12, p. 41A.

11. Kevorkian, J. "The fundus oculi and the determination of death." *Amercian Journal of Pathology* 32 (1956): 1253-67.

12. Kevorkian, J. "History of human dissection," *WSU MEdical Library* Ref. QM33.5 K4 1959.

13. Kevorkian, J. "Transfusion of postmortem human blood." *Am J. Clin Path* 1961 May: 35(5):413-419.

14. Kevorkian, J. "Mercury content of human tissues during the 20th Centry." *Am J. Public Health* 1972 Apr: 62(4):504-13.

15. Kevorkian, J. and Centro D. "Leiomyosarcoma of large arteries and veins." *Surgery* (March 1973) Vol. 73, No. 3, pp. 390-398.

16. Kevorkian, J. "A coherent grid system of coordinates for precise anatomical localization." *Anatomica Clinica* 1984; 6(3):183-93.

Endnotes

17. *Detroit Free Press Magazine* (18 March 1992), p. 24.

18. Newman, Steven. "Euthanasia: Orchestrating 'The Last Syllable of... Time. '" 53 *U. Pitt. L. Rev.* 153 (1991).

19. Kevorkian, *Prescription: Medicide*, pp. 195-196.

20. *Ibid.,* p. 221.

21. *Ibid.,* p. 222.

22. *Ibid.,* p. 214.

23. *Ibid.,* p. 225.

24. *Id.*

25. *Ibid.,* p. 222.

26. *Ibid.,* p. 224-225.

27. *Ibid.,* pp. 225-226.

28. *Id.*

29. *Ibid.,* pp. 226-227.

30. *Ibid.,* pp. 222-223.

31. *Ibid.,* p. 225.

32. *Ibid.,* p. 223.

33. *Ibid.,* p. 227.

34. *Ibid.,* p. 230.

35. *Ibid.,* p. 225.

36. *Ibid.*

37. Kevorkian, *Prescription: Medicide,* p. 93.

38. "Where you Stand on Physician-Assisted Suicide in Michigan." *The Advisor Newspaper* (19 October 1992): A5.

39. *In re Nancy Cruzan,* 110 S. Ct. 2841, Justice Scalia's concurring opinion at 2859.

Endnotes

40. Kevorkian, *Prescription: Medicide*, p. 234.

41. *Ibid.*, p. 94.

42. Humphry, Derek. *Final Exit*. Eugene, Oregon, The Hemlock Society.

43. "Where you Stand," *supra*.

44. Humphry, *supra*.

45. "Soundoff." *The Macomb Daily* (28 1992): Opinion Page.

46. Kevorkian, J. *Prescription: Medicide,* p. 193.

47. Letter to Editor, *Detroit Free Press* (09 November 1992): 6A.

48. "Assisted Suicide: A Matter of Compassion." *Detroit Free Press* (13 October 1992): Editorial Page.

49. *People v Roberts.* (1920), 178 N.W. 2d 690, 211 Mich.187, 13 A.L.R. 1253.

50. People v Campbell (1983), 335 N.W. 2d27, 124 Mich. App. 333

51. *People vs. Kevorkian,* Oakland County (Michigan) Circuit Court, Hon. David Breck's Opinion.

52. "Where you stand," *supra*.

53. Kevorkian, J. "Medicine, Ethics, and Execution by Lethal Injection." *Medicine and Law* (1985) 4:311.

54. "Speak Out." *The Advisor Newspaper* (24 October 1992): A4.

55. "Where You Stand," *supra*.

56. Letter to Editor. *Detroit Free Press* (08 November 1992).

57. Kevorkian, *Prescription: Medicide,* p. 241.

58. *Ibid.,* p. 203.

59. Kevorkian, J. Article. *American Journal of Forensic Psychiatry* (1992).

Index

Index

Index

Index

Index

Index

-Y-
Yeargain, Joseph 57

-Z-
Zalewski, Lt. Daniel 124
Zimmerman, Rev. Paul 178-179